RAILWAYS IN THE AUSTRIAN TIROL

Martin Bairstow

Published by Martin Bairstow, Fountain Chambers, Halifax, West Yorkshire
Printed by Hart & Clough Ltd, Summerville Road, Bradford

Introduction

Time passes so quickly and seven years have now elapsed since publication of 'Railways in the Bernese Oberland'. Sceptics said we were throwing our money away as nobody would buy a 'foreign' book. It hasn't been a best-seller but nor has it proved too much of a disaster. By the end of 1993, just under 1,700 copies had been sold out of the 2,000 printed. This is about half the quantity which one of our local titles might have achieved in the same timescale.

During the intervening time, I have toyed with the idea of another Continental title and here at last it is.

Hopefully, this book reflects some of the technical improvements which have been achieved since 'Railways in the Bernese Oberland'. Most obviously the use of some colour but also the better reproduction of black and white photographs.

The Austrian Tirol is an area frequented by British holidaymakers, a good proportion of who do make use of the local railways though not, it is feared, to the extent that tourists are dependent on rail travel in Switzerland. Clearly there is interest amongst British people in Austrian Railways as witness the formation in 1992 of the Austrian Railways Group which quickly gained a membership of over 100.

For the purpose of the book, the borders of the Tirol have been stretched a little so as to include the western ascent of the Arlberg which is actually in the province of Vorarlberg and to continue the Giselabahn to its junction with the Tauern Main Line at Schwarzach-St Veit which lies well within Salzburgerland. The Italian Südtirol, or Alto Adige, which was Austrian before 1919, is featured only in passing. This area is bilingual. Both Italian and German names appear on the maps but, the German names are used in the text for places south of the Brenner Pass.

Apart from this, there should not be too much problem with place names as on the whole we do not attempt to anglicise other people's towns and cities, except for the very well known. Only Munich and Vienna appear in the book and they are referred to consistently as München and Wien.

A glance at a relief map will confirm that the entire area featured in this book is mountainous. It follows that all the railways are heavily engineered, steeply graded and scenic.

For these qualities alone, the railways of the Tirol are of outstanding interest. But they also stand at the very centre of the European railway system. The mountains rule out high speed but in other respects they are at the forefront in the development of the railway industry.

Lines which were built more than a century ago to try and hold together the Habsburg Empire are now being adapted to accommodate the ever increasing traffic generated by the European Community. Fiscal measures are used to encourage freight on to the Railway. Passengers are sold an 'Environmental Ticket' to make rail more competitive.

The Tirolean Railways are not all international main lines. A network of local lines has also been retained much of it modernised but there is still room for some quaint survivors such as the century old rack locomotives pounding their way up from Jenbach to the Achensee.

Coverage of such a wide variety of lines can only be superficial in a publication of this size. It is hoped, none the less, that the book will serve as an introduction and guide to the railways of the Tirol maybe helping visitors to get more out of their trip, possibly tempting others to go for the first time.

Halifax, West Yorkshire
May 1994

Martin Bairstow

Tickets from the collection of Geoffrey Lewthwaite including one issued on 18 September 1938 to a member of the 'Wehrmacht'. The 'Schnellzugzuschlag' (fast train supplement) was issued on 17 August 1950. Supplements have now almost died out in Austria.

2

Austria

The Country . . .

The Republic of Austria dates from 1919 when the victorious Allies redrew the map of Europe after the First World War. Having dealt with Germany at Versailles, the peace negotiators moved on to nearby St Germain En Laye to conclude, on 10 September 1919, the treaty which confirmed the break up of the former Austro Hungarian Empire.

Previously Vienna had been the capital of an Empire embracing all of present day Austria, Hungary, the Czech Republic, Slovakia, Slovenia and Croatia along with parts of Poland, Romania and Italy, also the tragic state of Bosnia-Herzegovina which Austria had annexed in 1908. It was in the Bosnian capital Sarajevo that Archduke Franz Ferdinand, heir to the Austrian throne, was murdered on 28 June 1914 – the event which sparked off the First World War.

With an area of 32,368 square miles or 83,855 square km, much of it mountainous and a population (nowadays) of 7½ million, Austria comprises most, but by no means all, the German speaking parts of the former Empire. The Südtirol, part German and part Italian speaking, was ceded to Italy creating a frontier at the Brenner Pass. This was Italy's reward for having entered the War on the Allied side.

There might also have been a frontier at the Arlberg Tunnel. One of the supposed principles behind the peace settlement was self determination.

As long as Allied interests were not compromised, people could decide by referendum where the new boundaries would fall. In 1919, the citizens of Vorarlberg voted by a large majority to leave Austria and join Switzerland. Unfortunately the Swiss would not have them.

Austria was forbidden under the Treaty of St Germain En Laye from amalgamating with Germany but Hitler was Austrian and regarded the two countries as one. By the 'Anschluss' of March 1938, Austria was incorporated into Nazi Germany.

At the end of the Second World War, Austria was restored to its 1919 boundaries but occupied on a four power basis rather like Germany with Vienna, which lay within the Soviet zone, subject to separate four power control similar to that covering Berlin.

In 1955, the four powers were persuaded to withdraw on condition that Austria pledged itself to perpetual neutrality along the Swiss model.

Though neutral in the military sense, Austria became firmly allied to the west economically. Whilst the 'Cold War' continued, neutrality was thought to rule out membership of the European Community but since the fall of the Berlin Wall, Austria has entered into negotiations for entry into the EC.

It was the dismantling by Hungary of its part of the 'Iron Curtain' along the border with Austria in 1989 which played an important part in the collapse of Communism in Eastern Europe.

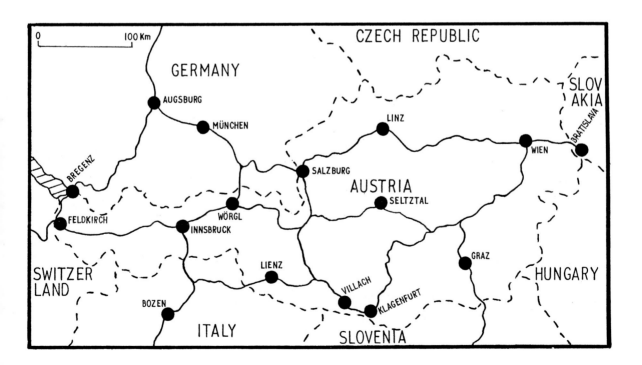

One of the few lines to have closed in the area covered by this book is the Innsbruck – Hall in Tirol Lokalbahn. Motor Coach No 1 is seen at the Solbad Hall terminus on 9 July 1969. It closed on 9 June 1974. *(G C Lewthwaite)*

Provided that this is followed by economic revival amongst Austria's eastern neighbours, then Vienna may once again find itself near the heart of Europe rather than the last outpost of the western sector which is what it has been for most of the past half century.

. . . and its Railways

The twin attractions of the rail travel in Austria are the magnificent scenery and the efficient system which receives strong backing from its Government. Closures have been isolated. There has never been anything like the systematic onslaught witnessed in the British Isles during the 1960s nor the turmoil in pursuit of political dogma which we are seeing now in the 1990s.

The Austrian Railways have much in common with their Swiss neighbours. The system is not as dense but Austria is a much larger country with only a slightly greater population than Switzerland. The Austrian Railways are by no means all electrified and there are only a few rack lines compared to the numerous examples in Switzerland.

The major part of the Austrian network is owned and operated by the Österreichische Bundesbahnen – the Austrian Federal Railways whose mileage includes a few narrow gauge lines mostly of 76cm. There are, in addition, a number of so called private railways, some of which are actually in local public ownership. These play a full part in the national network in terms of integrated ticketing and timetabling. Then there are the urban tramway networks in Graz, Linz and Innsbruck together with the extensive tram and metro system in Vienna.

There are also funiculars and lake steamers adding variety to the overall scene.

The Austrian Government pursues a number of policies aimed at maximising use of rail transport. Two of the most prominent features on the passenger side have been imported from Switzerland: the 'Taktfahrplan' and the 'Halbtaxabonnement'.

The nationwide regular interval timetable, or 'Taktfahrplan', introduced in Switzerland in 1982, arrived in Austria in 1991 under the title of 'Neue Austro Takt'. It has not yet penetrated every corner of the system but is built around a network of 'Inter City' trains running on seven routes at two hourly intervals. Most sections of line are served by two services thus giving an 'Inter City' train every hour in each direction. Local and semi fast trains then interconnect either hourly or two hourly. If the system is working, you should always pass the corresponding train in the opposite direction on or about the hour.

The Swiss 'Halbtaxabonnement' has come to Austria as 'Die Umwelt Ticket' – The Environmental Ticket. In Germany it is called 'Die Bahn Card'. All three German speaking countries have each adopted the universal half fare pass in order to make rail travel more competitive in relation to the private car.

The great problem is that, whilst motoring is very expensive, most of the costs are fixed regardless of mileage. The perceived cost of driving a car that extra hundred miles is only two or three gallons of petrol which is less than the price of a rail ticket.

To combat this the railway issues, for an annual fee, a pass which entitles the holder to half fares at all times. This puts the rail traveller in a similar position to the motorist. He has already paid his overheads and can now travel at relatively modest cost.

The 'Umwelt Ticket' cost 1,080 schillings (about £63) for a year in 1993 and gave half fare, without restriction, on the ÖBB, most private lines and ships on the Danube. Senior Citizens could acquire the same benefits for 240s but men have to wait until they are 65, women only till 60. There is also a facility for families.

Regular travellers may purchase a 'Bundesnetzkarte' covering the entire ÖBB plus most private lines for periods between a month and a year. For tourists who are not going to be there that long, there is the 'Rabbit Card' which is a 'Bundesnetzkarte' valid on any four days within a period of ten days. In 1993, this cost 1,130 schillings (about £65) or 700 schillings for persons under 26 which is good value for people in their early 20s but rather less so for younger children who might have expected to pay half price. First class is also available but is wasted on many branch and local trains which only have second class accommodation. A photo identity card is required (ie passport). In practice only a minority of ticket examiners ever ask to see it. I did ascertain that it is all right for an accompanied child to rely on his/her name in parents passport even though there is no separate photograph.

RABBIT CARD

BAIRSTON JOHN
Name

Lichtbildausweis erforderlich/Identity-card necessary

Shortly before going to press, I learnt that Rabbit Cards had been abolished at the end of 1993. In their place are four 'Österreich Puzzle' tickets also valid four days out of ten at 990 schillings second class. Each ticket covers a region of Austria — North, South, East and West. The West ticket covers Nord Tirol, Salzburgerland, Vorarlberg and Ost Tirol.

The 1993/94 ÖBB annual timetable runs to 1,046 pages and cost 100 schilllings (£6). It covers private lines, ships, funiculars, cable cars etc plus urban tram and bus services. Other buses are contained in a similar national publication and bus information is generally available at railway stations.

2095.001 approaching Mühlbach with a Krimml train on 23 August 1987. *(John Holroyd)*

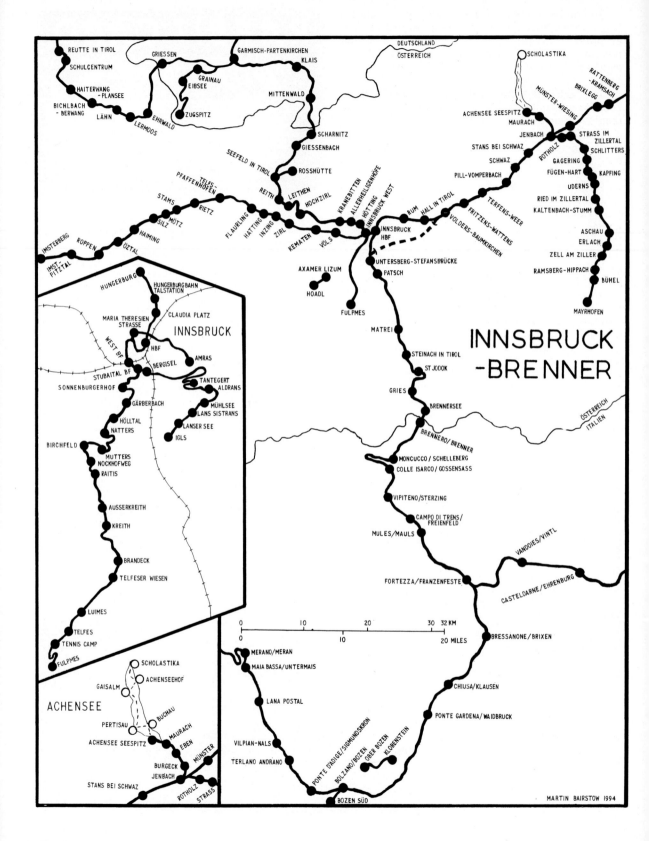

INNSBRUCK
-BRENNER

INNSBRUCK

ACHENSEE

MARTIN BAIRSTOW 1994

6

A Living Railway

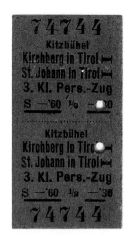

Kirchberg in Tirol on 21 August 1993. The two telephone kiosks mentioned in the text were installed outside the station a few days later.
(Martin Bairstow)

It is quarter past nine at the end of what has been another disappointing day, weather wise. Our evening stroll has taken us, dodging the puddles, towards the station.

Kirchberg in Tirol is only a small town, little more than a village but the resident population is swollen during both Summer and Winter seasons by the influx of tourists. Possibly a majority come by car, especially from centres of population in Germany which are fairly close at hand. Some arrive by rail, some by coach and others, including a lot of British visitors, reach the Tirol via Salzburg Airport. Unless these people hire a car or rely on coach trips for all their outings, they need public transport for getting around. Hence the volume of passenger business at Kirchberg Station is out of proportion to the number of local inhabitants. This is why Kirchberg is an 'Inter City' station with both express and local trains every hour in each direction.

The main building is a single storey affair of modern appearance somewhat in contrast to the traditional two storey structures elsewhere on the line which have living accommodation upstairs. A plaque affixed to a nearby building records that it was destroyed during the Second World War and rebuilt afterwards. This may afford a clue to the fate of the original station.

Outside is a taxi rank, bus stop, car park for rail customers and two telephone kiosks installed whilst we were there.

Inside the booking hall cum waiting room we find the place well lit and scrupulously clean. The buffet and sweetshop/newspaper kiosk have closed for the night but the ticket office is still open. The shutters are down at the adjacent parcels/luggage office but there is a buzzer to press which would summon the sole incumbent from the booking office.

All is fairly quiet but the absence of customers does not allow the man to put his feet up because the booking clerk is also a signalman. In fact, as 'Fahrdienstleiter', his prime function is train regulation. Selling tickets is secondary and there is a separate clerk for this purpose during the daytime. It is quite common in Austria for the booking office to contain a signal panel or even a manual frame. At Kirchberg there are two signal boxes located at either end of the station layout controlling the points, signals and level crossings but the block instruments are in the 'Fahrdienstleitung' which doubles up as ticket office. The 'Fahrdienstleiter' sets the route through the station and operates the block instruments to the adjacent stations in each direction. In doing so, he gives an electrical release to the two signal boxes enabling them to set the necessary points and signals.

Other facilities around the open plan ticket hall include telephones, clean toilets and timetables which are displayed on posters around the waiting area in one corner where there are tables and chairs.

Automatic sliding glass doors lead onto platform 1 which is on the eastbound loop line normally used only by local trains. The platform is too short for the longer express trains which use the island platform Nos 2 and 3 served by the main lines in each direction. Track 4, the westbound loop has no platform. All four tracks are signalled for reversible working, though right hand running is the normal mode.

The island platform is reached by a subway which is clean, draught free thanks to sliding glass doors and adorned with posters offering such attractions as special trains over the Iron Mountain, the former rack operated line between Vordernberg and Eisenerz in Steiermark.

At 21.21 an empty class 4020 three coach emu passes through in the direction of Wörgl.

The loudspeaker then announces the imminent arrival of Inter City 'Pongau', the 21.23 to Salzburg. This would normally come from Innsbruck but during the Summer of 1993, the two hourly service on Inter City route No 2 Innsbruck – Zell am See – Salzburg – Linz – Wien West was curtailed to start from Wörgl because of engineering work. 'Pongau' only goes as far as Salzburg because it is so late in the day.

All 'Inter City' trains have names. 'Pongau' is an area through which the train will pass when it joins the Tauern Main Line at Schwarzach – St Veit.

If we want to know the train formation, we look at the 'Wagenstandanzeiger' which appears on all main line platforms consisting of a picture diagram of the various trains indicating the origin, destination and class of each carriage. This enables passengers to wait at the correct position on the platform and is particularly useful for trains which split into different portions. In this case, all ten coaches are going to Salzburg.

1044.222 is in charge of the 'Pongau'. A handful of passengers join and a number alight including a contingent of brightly coloured, noisy individuals who must have cleaned out the 'off licence' in Wörgl. This is a comparatively rare phenomenon in Kirchberg. They disperse quickly but as they go, they drown the sound of the approaching 21.25 local, a class 4030 three car emu dating from the early 1960s, which slips into platform 3 to deposit and pick up two or three customers.

Each departure, and indeed each passing train, is observed by the 'Fahrdienstleiter' standing to attention outside his office and always wearing his red topped cap. It is he who gives the starting signal to the driver not the train conductor (Zugführer) who only performs that function at unstaffed stations.

Not all local trains are emus. Three hours earlier I arrived at Kirchberg by the 15.13 ex Salzburg which was formed of three coaches plus a mail van hauled by 1042.043. I had joined at Eschenau, an unstaffed halt in a gorge by the Salzach east of Zell am See. The 1 hour 40 minute journey had taken me through the mountains – indeed on this day through the clouds as well. The main flow of traffic had been commuters who boarded at Zell am See, most of whom had got off by Steinberg.

As the tail light of 4030.302 disappears into the distance, three powerful headlights appear. Gradually they draw closer but are switched off on entering the station, which seems to be normal practice, in order to reveal electric centre cab loco No 1063.049 at the head of just one container wagon travelling east.

The next train is the 21.37 'Regional Zug' all stations to Bischofshofen, the last eastbound local of the day. It is another 4030 unit which slips quietly through the eastbound loop calling at platform 1. The 'Taktfahrplan' is almost perfectly symmetrical. The westbound local was at 25 past the hour, the eastbound is at 23 minutes to. The expresses are at 23 past and 22 to the hour when it is Inter City Line 2 and 18 past, 17 to the hour for line 7. With a two hourly regular interval, you should always pass the corresponding train in the opposite direction more or less on the hour – and also at half past if it is an hourly interval service.

Whether we consult the timetable, or just rely on our calculator, the next train must be the 21.43 towards Innsbruck. This is the 'Bergisel', named after a mountain overlooking Innsbruck, which left Graz at 16.40 and is travelling beyond Innsbruck to give a last service to Landeck on the Arlberg Main

A good deal of traditional freight is still carried by rail in Austria. Bales of straw are unloaded in the yard at Kirchberg in Tirol, August 1993.   *(Martin Bairstow)*

Line. The 'Transalpin' set will then start from Landeck the next morning at 06.18 as the 'Dachstein' back to Graz.

Once we have watched the 'Bergisel' depart, we have seen the four passenger trains in the hourly sequence. We begin to think of wandering back towards the hotel but we hear the warning sound as the level crossing barriers go down again. 1044.111 goes through with an eastbound freight. It really is time we got back but we still see two more trains. As we walk along the road towards the level crossing and town centre, 1010.010 thunders past with a long eastbound freight. We are unable to identify the loco which passes behind on a freight in the other direction. It is 21.55. In ³/₄ hour we have witnessed nine train movements. The station will be open for another 2¹/₂ hours. There are two more trains booked to stop, the final one at quarter past midnight. Kirchberg booking office will then reopen for business at 04.45 the next morning and that applies seven days a week.

This had been Wednesday. We repeated our evening stroll the following Saturday when we found two small parties standing at different points on the island platform congregating around piles of luggage. All appeared to be speaking Dutch (or Flemish).

They had evidently consulted the 'Wagenstandanzeiger' to determine the relative position of the Utrecht and Oostende coaches on the Saturdays only 21.38 overnight express. This runs weekly from May to September starting from Zell am See and again from 25 December (they do run trains on Christmas Day on the Continent) until early April when it acquires the name 'Ski Express'.

Scheduled departure from Kirchberg was 21.38 at which hour, German loco 110 125 drew into platform 3 at the head of three German and three Belgian coaches, all second class, two couchettes and one ordinary corridor carriage for each destination. The destination boards on the Belgian stock proclaimed 'Oostende for London'. We speculated how long it would take us to get home by this service compared to our own travel plans which involved a flight from Salzburg the following afternoon. Sadly rail is not really credible for journeys between the UK and the Alps. It could become so if the Channel Tunnel is exploited fully but we will have to wait and see how much change this will bring.

For these Dutch and Belgian holidaymakers returning home, the train probably was preferable to some of the alternatives like overnight on a bus. On this occasion they got off to a bad start as it stood in platform 3 until 21.55 waiting for the 21.43 'Bergisel' to pass and then to clear the block section. This duly arrived 'wrong road' in platform 2, a few minutes late demonstrating both the flexibility of reversible working and the principle of giving priority to the regular interval 'Inter City' over the international couchette service.

4030.303 (with 6030 driving trailer leading) stands in platform 1 at Kirchberg on 25 August 1993 waiting to return to Wörgl. Most local trains which normally run through to Salzburg, were suspended between Kirchberg and Kitzbühel on this day due to track work.
(Martin Bairstow)

1020.008 sets off back towards Saalfelden having detached from a heavy freight which it had banked to Kirchberg which at 820 metres is one of the two summits of the Giselabahn. It is about to pass Stellwerke 1, the signal box at the east end of the layout. *(Martin Bairstow)*

1044.047 thunders through Kirchberg with the Inter City 'Hahnenkamm' for Wien West on 21 August 1993. There are two consecutive 'Inter City' trains eastbound in the morning which stop at Fieberbrunn rather than Kirchberg creating something of a gap in the service. *(Martin Bairstow)*

The Nordtiroler Bahn

Innsbruck-Wörgl-Kufstein

The oldest railway in the Tirol is the 73km route from Innsbruck to Kufstein, just short of the German border.

Given the technology of the 1850s, it was quite logical that the first railway should follow the relatively easy route through the Inn Valley even though this meant that the Tirol would be connected to the rest of the Austrian rail system only via Bavaria which was then an independent kingdom. It became part of Germany in 1870.

The maximum gradient is 1 in 300. The line descends towards Kufstein which at 499 metres above sea level is just 76 metres lower than Innsbruck.

The Nordtiroler Staatsbahn was planned and built by the Austrian Government in conjunction with the Maximiliansbahn of the Imperial Bavarian Railways. This continued the route 32 km into Bavarian territory as far as Rosenheim which lies on the main line between München and Salzburg. The joint project was agreed in a treaty between Austria and Bavaria in June 1851. Work began in 1854.

The Nordtirolerbahn opened on 24 November 1858, by which time the Bavarian line had been in operation for just over three months. The Government offered a concession over the Nordtirolerbahn to the Südbahn Company as an incentive to get the Brenner project under way.

The route between Innsbruck and Kufstein had been built throughout as single track. It was doubled in the years 1889-1891 with left hand running which still prevails on this line and on the Brenner.

Electrification followed after the First World War. In July 1920, the newly formed Austrian Government announced a programme of electrification covering all lines of the Federal Railways west of Salzburg. Work on the Innsbruck to Kufstein section began in 1925 and was completed on 9 July 1927. The first German electric train arrived in Kufstein just six days later enabling through electric working to commence between Innsbruck and München. The Südbahn had been merged into the Federal Railways in 1924.

Although there has been an all Austrian route from Innsbruck to Salzburg since 1875, it is much shorter and faster to travel via Kufstein then through Germany.

The route between Kufstein and Salzburg is one of four 'Korridorstrecke' over which internal Austrian trains travel. This is by far the most important one. There are two more in the Tirol, one over German and one over Italian territory. The fourth example is in the east of Austria where trains pass through Hungary.

DB 'Trans-Europ-Express' 'Mediolanum' passing Jenbach en route from München to Milano on 18 August 1970. One way to overcome the voltage change at Brenner was to run diesel throughout.
(Douglas Butterfield)

A class 4041 emu of 1929 vintage leaves Innsbruck Hauptbahnhof as the 9.52 to Wörgl on 26 August 1970. A three coach set is now preserved from this extinct class.　　　　*(Douglas Butterfield)*

1044.216, passing Jenbach on 21 August 1993 with a 'rollende strasse' lorry train for the Brenner line. The Zillertalbahn is on the right. Diesel shunter 2062.007 sits in the yard.　　　　*(Martin Bairstow)*

Wörgl Station looking north in August 1973. It has recently been rebuilt with more substantial platforms. 4061-20 is now 1046.020. Built 1956-59, these locomotives were originally numbered in the emu series because they have baggage accommodation but later on they decided that they were locomotives after all.
(Stuart Baker)

The distance between Innsbruck and Salzburg direct is 193 km against 255 km via Zell am See and Bischofshofen. The journey time is just under two hours compared to almost 3½ hours by the all Austrian route. Normal fares are calculated as if travelling via Zell am See. 'Rabbit Cards' etc. are valid for through travel via the 'Korridorstrecke'.

Until 1982, trains had to reverse in Rosenheim Station, a procedure helped by the employment of push-pull 'Trans Alpin' sets. The 1976 summer timetable shows five trains per day taking this route, all of them through to Wien, some having come through from Switzerland. Journey time between Innsbruck and Salzburg was 2¼ hours. The reversal in Rosenheim was eliminated when the Deutsche Bundesbahn built a single track spur, 2 km in length south of Rosenheim specially for this traffic.

Today the 'Trans Alpin' sets have been cascaded on to other routes and all services via the 'Korridorstrecke' are loco hauled. There is a two hourly 'Inter City' service from Bregenz to Wien Westbahnhof. The first leaves Innsbruck at 7.02 and the last at 19.02.

Over and above this, there are three 'Euro City' trains, the 'Franz Schubert', 'Transalpin' and the 'Maria Theresia' respectively at 11.24, 13.24 and 17.24 from Innsbruck. These are through from Switzerland to Wien. Finally there is the 'Wiener Symphoniker' which is through from Bregenz to Wien (19.56 ex Innsbruck). This is described as a 'Super City' which is basically a 'Euro City' running through only one country.

'Euro City' trains carry a supplementary fare in first class for which customers get extra facilities such as waiter service at their seats but in Austria there is no supplement in second class. They have the best carriages though not necessarily any better than 'Inter City'. They claim 'outstanding punctuality' and certainly are afforded priority at passing loops and overtaking points.

Kufstein is also served by trains at two hourly intervals coming from Italy via Brenner, Innsbruck, Wörgl and going on to Rosenheim and München.

The section between Innsbruck and Wörgl serves as two main lines rolled into one as both east-west and north-south routes share this common bit of track. Midway along this stretch is Jenbach, the only station in Austria to incorporate three gauges within the same station. Trains on the metre gauge Achenseebahn and the 76 cm gauge Zillertalbahn begin their journeys on opposite sides of the standard gauge main line. Both branches feature later in the book. They add colour to the railway scene but it is on the main line that the heavy traffic runs. Stand on the bridge at the west end and you won't have to wait long to see a train movement, passenger or freight with German as well as Austrian locomotives and with rolling stock from all over Europe. I have witnessed two eastbound freights taking refuge in the loops on both sides of the main line then, after passenger trains have gone in each direction, they have set off simultaneously in the direction of Innsbruck which they can do when the line is signalled for reversible working.

There is an hourly local service from Innsbruck to Wörgl generally worked by an emu of either class 4030 or the newer 4020. There is also an hourly 'Inter City' on this section bound for the Zell am See route. This is worked alternately by a 'Trans Alpin' set and by a loco hauled formation. This service calls at Jenbach (which is not served by trains to Salzburg via Kufstein). Between Wörgl and Kufstein there is an hourly local emu connecting with the aforementioned express from Innsbruck.

6030.04 (now 6030.304) prepares to leave Kufstein with a local for Wörgl on 24 August 1971. The Class 6030 vehicle is the driving trailer. The motor coach at the other end will always carry the corresponding number in the 4030 series. These units were built 1956-59.

(Douglas Butterfield)

Prien Am Chiemsee lies partway between Kufstein and Salzburg on the 'Korridorstrecke'. A class 1044 heads east with a 'Rollende Strasse'. A dmu comprising two 4 wheel 'railbuses' waits departure on the branch to Aschau. These used to be very common on the DB and ÖBB.

(Martin Bairstow)

What draws connoisseurs to Prien is the Chiemseebahn, a standard gauge steam tramway which runs down from the main line station to the steamer terminal at Stock, about 2km away. The line has one steam loco, built 1889 and a diesel built in the style of a steam tram engine. There is no mistaking which loco is storming out of Stock taking a run at the gradient on a very wet 28 August 1993.

(Martin Bairstow)

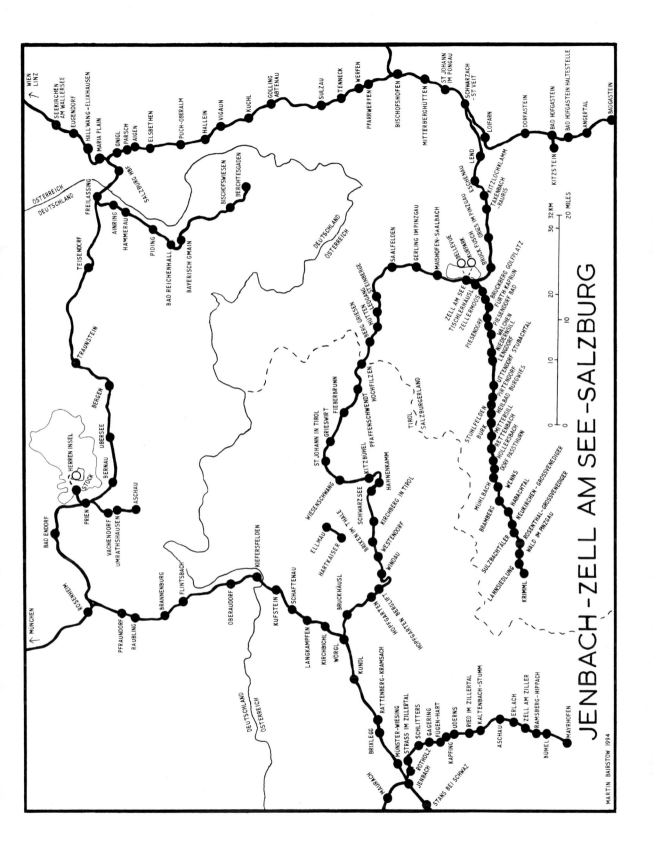

JENBACH–ZELL AM SEE–SALZBURG

MARTIN BAIRSTOW 1994

15

Over the Brenner Pass

ÖBB 1670.01 is ready to pilot DB 110.476 from Innsbruck up to Brenner with an express from Dortmund to Verona on 26 August 1970.   *(Douglas Butterfield)*

The Ötztaler, Stubaier and Zillertaler Alpen together mark the border between the Nord and Südtirol. The various peaks rise to over 3,500 metres. They rarely fall below 2,500. Together they mark the watershed between the Inn, which flows eventually into the Black Sea, and the Eisack which finds its way to the Adriatic.

At 1,370 metres above sea level, the Brenner pass offered the one obvious route by which a railway might penetrate this otherwise very inhospitable terrain. This was the route which the Romans had used to build the 'Via Claudia' around 200A.D. More recently in 1772, the Empress Maria Theresia had ordered the construction of a new 'Kaiser Strasse' over the Brenner Pass to link up with her more southerly domains.

Innsbruck enjoyed rail access from Wien and Salzburg from 1858. Further south, the Lombardy – Venetian Railway reached Bozen in 1859.

The Austrian Government offered to transfer the state owned Nordtiroler Bahn to the Lombardy – Venetian Company in 1858 if it would accept the concession to build the intervening section between Innsbruck and Bozen. The new enterprise was known briefly as the Imperial State Lombardian, Venetian and Central Italian Railway.

If the aim was partly strategic, then time was running out for Austria which lost Venetia in 1859

and Lombardy in 1866 to the cause of Italian unification. The Italians took over the railways in their new territory. The company which was to build the Brenner Railway then became the Imperial Southern Railway – the Südbahn.

Work began in February 1864. Up to 20,000 workers were employed on the project. Over 200 of them died from illness or accident. Many of the workers were Italians who left for home during the war with Italy from 20 June to 12 August 1866.

Despite this and many natural obstacles, the line was ready for a trial run on 25 July 1867. It opened on 17 August without ceremony because Austria was mourning the murdered Emperor Maximilian of Mexico, brother of Kaiser Franz Josef.

The line opened as single track but was doubled between Innsbruck and Brenner within a year.

With the transfer of the Südtirol from Austria to Italy at the end of the First World War, the railway from Brenner to Bozen passed to the Italian State Railways (FS). The remaining Austrian part of the Südbahn from Kufstein to Brenner was merged into Austrian Federal Railways in 1924.

The Austrian and Italian authorities were agreed on the need to electrify the Brenner Line but they had different views as to the system. Austria was committed to 15,000 volts a.c. and wanted to carry this system as far as Bozen. Italy was experimenting with a three phase system at 3,600 volts and they wanted to run through to Innsbruck. Neither side was prepared to give way.

On 6 October 1928, the Austrian electrification reached Brennersee station. By the following year Italian three phase locos were running into Brenner but the short section over the border still had to be worked by steam until 1934 when the Austrian wires were extended into Brenner station.

By 1939, the Italians had tired of the three phase system and were about to convert their side of the Brenner to 3,000 volts d.c. when the Second World War broke out. Conversion was delayed until 1965.

The Brenner Route carried very heavy traffic during the Second World War but was badly damaged towards the end of the conflict. The through route was not restored until May 1947.

The line climbs 796 metres in the 38km between Innsbruck and Brenner. Except between Matrei and Steinach where the route is comparatively level, the whole journey is close to the 1 in 40 ruling gradient.

Where the main valley, the Wipptal, becomes too steep, south of Steinach, the railway makes a detour up the side valley, the Schmirntal, in order to achieve a horseshoe curve.

There is a similar but much longer horseshoe on the south side where the railway takes a detour up the Pflerschtal. The stations at Schellerberg and Gossensass, 9 km apart by rail and height difference of 139 metres are separated by only 1.5km as the crow flies.

On both sides of the Brenner Pass, the scenery is dominated by the autobahn which was built between 1959 and 1969. Although no fan of motorway architecture, it is hard not to be impressed by the scale of some of the structures.

Local passenger trains leave Innsbruck for Brenner at 3 minutes past most hours but there are some two hour intervals. Express trains are at rather more erratic intervals. Austrian tickets are valid to Brenner station which is just inside Italy.

Taking the Brenner line out of Innsbruck on 27 August 1970. The Arlberg route has just branched to the right. The Brenner Autobahn is prominent.
(Douglas Butterfield)

1670.15 and 1010.05 passing Unterberg-Stefansbrücke with the Alpen Express on 24 August 1970 when the line was still semaphore signalled.
(Douglas Butterfield)

1044.075 calls at Steinach in Tirol with a local from Brenner to Innsbruck. The autobahn dominates the skyline. *(Martin Bairstow)*

Exterior view of the station at Steinach in Tirol. *(Martin Bairstow)*

Brennersee, the last station in Austria now unstaffed was for a brief time the limit of the 15,000 volt a.c. electrification. *(John Holroyd)*

E633.002 waits for business at the Italian end of Brenner station on 11 June 1991. Note the bilingual signs. *(Martin Bairstow)*

'Die Rollende Strasse'

The development of the European Community has greatly increased the volume of goods travelling between member states. Switzerland and (so far) Austria are not members but their territory must be crossed by traffic going from Germany to Italy. One of the main transit routes is from Kufstein to Brenner.

If transit traffic is carried in heavy lorries on the autobahn, then the Austrians (or Swiss) will just get the bill for road repairs not to mention constant pressure for road widening in order that their own citizens may also get a look in driving along these roads.

A proportion of transit traffic goes all the way from Northern Europe to Italy by rail. Usually the German loco stays on the train for the 110km trip through Austria. It may also have an Austrian pilot loco for the climb up to the Brenner Pass.

There is plenty of transit traffic in road lorries. For both economic and environmental reasons, Austria wants as much of this as possible to pass through its territory by rail. The method is the "Rollende Strasse" which is a lorry carrying train.

Use of this facility is encouraged by taxes on transit traffic, by a limit on the size of lorries allowed to cross Austria and by a ban on lorry movement at night. On the positive side, there is relief from Customs checks and associated paperwork for

vehicles which are carried by rail direct from Germany to Italy. If they do not touch Austrian roads, then they are not regarded as having entered Austria for Customs purposes.

The number of lorry movements conveyed by train over the Brenner rose four fold from about 25,000 in 1980 to 100,000 in 1990. The rise is set to continue as Austria has declared the intention virtually to eliminate heavy transit lorries from the Brenner Autobahn.

This requires major investment to increase the capacity of the Brenner Railway. The ÖBB has enlarged clearances to accommodate lorries 4.05 metres high. This work has to be carried out with minimal interruption to traffic. They cannot just close the line every Sunday as an organisation nearer to home might do. In 1985, the 176 metre Patscher Tunnel was widened. First one track was removed then the other one slewed to allow trains to pass slowly through the middle. No explosives were allowed because of the proximity to the foundation of the massive Europa Bridge on the autobahn.

The FS has been slower than the ÖBB in carrying out similar work on the south side of the pass. In 1990 a service of up to eight trains per day for 4.05m high lorries introduced between Ingolstadt in Bavaria and Brennersee, the last stop in Austria. At that time it could not go any further because the FS

The environmentally friendly (or Umweltfreundlich) way to carry juggernauts. Messrs Pierer take to the rails at Salzburg on 2 July 1992.
(David Beeken)

could only accommodate lorries up to 3.6 metres.

All this traffic has hitherto had to pass through the bottleneck at Innsbruck but 1994 sees the opening of the 13km avoiding line. Almost entirely in tunnel this connects the Nordtirolerbahn with the Brenner Line. There is a 450 metre long bridge over the Inn immediately after the junction near Volders – Baumkirchen and then it disappears into tunnel.

The change of locomotive at Brenner is a time consuming exercise. The arriving engine must come into the station with its pantograph down and then be rescued by a shunter which draws it forward then pushes it back to its own end of the station where it can resume contact with the wires. Dual (or even triple) voltage locomotives are used elsewhere in Europe. The ÖBB has now developed the class 1822 'Brennerlok' in conjunction with the DB and FS. Up to 80 may be built eventually to handle traffic through from München to Verona.

The ultimate solution to the ever increasing volume of transit traffic would be the Brenner Base Tunnel. Like the parallel Gotthard and Lötschberg Base Tunnel projects in Switzerland, this has been talked about for a long time.

The ÖBB has made provision in the Innsbruck avoiding tunnel for direct connection into a Brenner Base Route which would go all the way to Bozen either via Meran with five tunnels totalling 68km or by an alignment close to the present route with a 60km deep level tunnel. The Italians have a more modest plan for a shorter tunnel at a higher level connecting Matrei with Sterzing.

In the meantime the FS is going ahead with cut offs between Brenner and Gossensass and between Waidbruck and Kardaun, the latter involving 8km of new alignment mainly in tunnel.

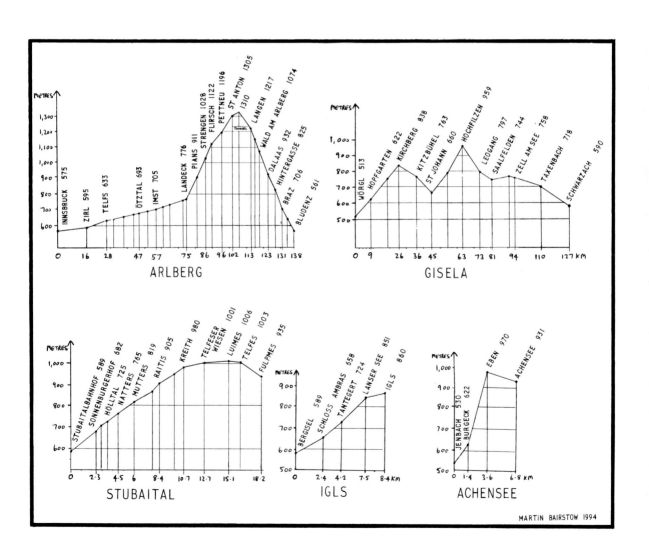

MARTIN BAIRSTOW 1994

Ost Tirol and the Pustertal

In 1974, the F S was still working steam on local traffic between Franzenfeste and Innichen. Two class 741 2-8-0s with Franco Crosti boilers are seen at Bruneck. *(Iain Parsons)*

One of the more protracted Inter City journeys available in Austria is that afforded by the 'Pustertal' (or Val Pusteria in Italian). This train leaves Wien Südbahnhof at 7.22 and reaches Innsbruck at 17.08, a journey of 9¹/₄ hours which is almost double the time taken by a 'Euro City' from Wien Westbahnhof to Innsbruck direct via Salzburg.

The 'Pustertal' takes its name from the valley which connects Lienz, the capital of Ost Tirol with Brixen on the south side of the Brenner.

When the railway opened through the Pustertal, it was of great strategic significance. In 1858 the Südbahn had been granted the concession to build a line from Villach through Lienz to Brixen but finance was not forthcoming and the scheme made no progress. But in 1866, war broke out between Austria and Germany and this caused Austria to lose the rail link between Innsbruck and Salzburg which passed through German territory.

This focused the attention of the Austrian Government onto the proposed Pustertalbahn which would provide an all Austrian route between the capital and Innsbruck. The Government came up with some finance. The planned connection with the Brenner Line at Brixen was amended in favour of a junction at Franzenfeste facing northwards.

The line was completed on 30 November 1871 and for a brief time it did provide the only rail link between the Austrian capital and the Tirol. This vital function was diluted with completion of the Giselabahn from Salzburg to Wörgl in 1875.

The appearance in 1919 of an international border between the Ost and Südtirol did little to prevent the Pustertalbahn from declining into a comparative backwater. Although the last station in Austria is at Weitlanbrunn, the ÖBB actually runs a further 10km as far as Innichen.

With the completion of electrification from Lienz to Franzenfeste in May 1989, the ÖBB ac and the FS dc wires now meet or at least come close together at this station. Electrification east of Lienz had been switched on two years earlier.

The single track Pustertal line begins at a junction 6km north west of Spital – Millstättersee where the Tauern Main Line leaves the valley of the River Drau and begins its assault on the mountains. The Pustertalbahn, which is older, continues with the Drau all the way to its source near Toblach which is the summit of the line and the watershed between the Drau, which flows eventually into the Black Sea and the Rienz which flows westwards through Pustertal to join the Eisack at Brixen, eventually finding its way into the Adriatic. The railway crosses the Eisack by a bridge 190 metres in length just before the final curve which leads into the junction with the Brenner Line at Franzenfeste,

'Neue Austro Takt' does not appear to have reached the thinly populated Osttirol. There are 14 departures per day from Spittal – Millstättersee, three of which run Mondays to Fridays only. These mostly call at all stations and terminate at Lienz. The exception is the 'Pustertal', the line's one Inter City train, through from Wien Südbahnhof. This continues semi-fast right through to Innsbruck. It loses all but three of its carriages at Lienz and changes to an Italian electric loco at Innichen only to change back again at Brenner.

There is a local service of seven trains daily between Lienz and Innichen. Two of these, at 5.30 and 18.28, also a third on Fridays and Saturdays only at 11.37 are the 'Korridorzüge', which run through from Lienz to Innsbruck – non-stop between Innichen and Brenner. To avoid changing engines, they are still worked throughout by ÖBB diesels of class 2043. It is possible that in future they could be handled by dual voltage class 1822 'Brenner Loks' if these are not too preoccupied with freight.

The 'Korridorzüge' run under a treaty signed in Paris in 1946 maintaining a historical link between the capitals of the Nord and Ost Tirol. The through journey time 3 1/4 to 3 1/2 hours may seem slow but the road journey would also be difficult. The quickest route would be to follow the railway.

The return trains leave Innsbruck at 7.10, 13.56 (Saturdays only), 14.48 (Fridays only) and 17.03.

This last one serves also as a commuter train from Innsbruck and sets off with seven coaches, a diesel at the front and an electric at the back which will come off at Brenner along with half the carriages.

ÖBB tickets, Rabbit Cards etc. are valid on the 'Korridorzüge' but not on the Inter City 'Pustertal' between Innichen and Brenner for which an Italian fare must be paid. This will not break the bank however as Italian fares are amongst the lowest in Europe. In 1993 we managed a round trip from Kirchberg via Schwarzach – St Veit, the Tauern Tunnel, Spittal – Millstättersee, the 'Pustertal' right through to Innsbruck and, finally, the 'Grimming' back to base.

By 1987, the wires were up but not yet energised leaving the F S local service at Bruneck in the hands of Fiat dmu 668.1715.
(John Holroyd)

Close up of 741.388 at Bruneck. The chimney was part way along the boiler on the right hand side rather than in the more conventional position. British Railways had ten class 9F locos equipped in this manner.   *(Iain Parsons)*

Fiat built F S dmu at Toblach in 1974   *(Iain Parsons)*

Italian d.c. loco E 652.063 backs onto the Inter City 'Pustertal' at Innichen/San Candido on 23 August 1993. The Austrian loco, which has been hauled away by a diesel shunter, is just visible in the distance. E 424.290 stands at the head of an FS local train. The view is from the leading coach of the 'Pustertal' looking west.   *(Philip Bairstow)*

Both the ÖBB and F S sections of the Pustertalbahn have been electrically operated since 1989. 1042.628 has run round its train at Lienz and is ready to return to Spittal-Millstättersee. The class 4030 unit is bound for Innichen. *(Martin Bairstow)*

Typical of the larger station buildings in Pustertal, Kleblach-Lind looking west. By this stage, the line has left the Ost Tirol and entered the province of Kärnten. *(Martin Bairstow)*

Die Gisela Bahn

Wörgl – Zell am See – Salzburg

The wars between Prussia and Austria in 1866 and between Prussia and France in 1870/71 bound Bavaria and other hitherto independent states into the Prussian dominated German Empire.

The new Germany was, at first, hostile to Austria which had previously exercised influence in southern Germany and which might have entertained ambitions of its own to bring about a united Germany under control from Wien.

In those circumstances, it was most unsatisfactory, even dangerous, to have the only rail link between the Tirol and the rest of Austria, dependent on passage through German territory. The Pustertalbahn, then under construction and opened in 1871 did give Innsbruck an all Austrian link with the capital albeit quite an indirect one. All of which added impetus to plans for the Salzburg – Tiroler Bahn.

A line was already authorised between Salzburg and Hallein. In 1872 this was incorporated into the concession granted to the Kaiserin Elisabeth Eisenbahngesellschaft (Empress Elizabeth Railway Company or 'Giselabahn' for short) to complete lines between Salzburg, Bischofshofen and Wörgl, also eastwards from Bischofshofen to Selzthal.

Despite its imperial name, the Giselabahn was a private (as opposed to a state owned) company but it did enjoy some state financial support in order to get it built within the three years specified in the concession. Having been directly involved in building the early railways, the Government had, since the late 1850s preferred to grant concessions to independent companies.

Helped by an influx of Italian labour, this target was achieved. The line from Salzburg to Wörgl opened throughout on 31 July 1875. This was despite a landslip near Taxenbach which made necessary a 300 metre tunnel. This could not be finished until May 1878 but a temporary track was built round the obstacle in the meantime.

The Kaiserin Elisabeth Company was absorbed into the state owned Imperial Railways in 1882. This followed a change in policy under which most of the main lines, but not the Südbahn, were brought back into public ownership.

Conversion from single to double track took place in the years 1912 to 1915, just in time for the upsurge in military traffic to the southern front occasioned by Italy joining the First World War against Austria and Germany.

The route was electrified between Wörgl and Saalfelden in 1928 and through to Salzburg by the summer of 1929.

The mountain section of the Giselabahn begins at Wörgl where the train leaves the Inn Valley and the line to Kufstein by a sharp right hand curve just

1042.060 calls at Kirchberg with the 15.13 Salzburg to Wörgl stopping train on 20 August 1993. Most locals are multiple unit operated but this one conveys an extra mail van.   *(Martin Bairstow)*

east of the station. The train runs on the right hand track as is the practice on the majority of double track lines in Austria.

In complete contrast to the fast run from Innsbruck, the train now has to negotiate gradients of up to 1 in 44 on a route which twists and twinds with the contours. Between Bruckhäusl and Hopfgarten, the line passes through a narrow gorge but perhaps the most memorable feature of this route is the horseshoe encountered between Hopfgarten Berglift and Windau stations. The only way that the line can get across the Windauer Ache is to continue southwards to a point where it is narrow enough to cross then, having turned through 180 degrees, climb steeply up the other side before eventually striking off in an easterly direction towards Westendorf. Given the frequency of passenger and freight trains over this line, there is a good chance of viewing a train, travelling apparently in parallel, on the other side of the valley. Returning from Innsbruck to Kirchberg by the 17.20 'Grimming', a Trans Alpin set, I had a superb view, with the evening light in just the right direction, of a freight descending the other side with a 1020 on each end. We passed just on the viaduct over the Windauer Ache as both trains swung round the head of the loop.

There is a footpath alongside the railway between Westendorf and the first summit station at Kirchberg in Tirol making lineside photography quite easy.

A second horseshoe is negotiated when the line performs a circle round the town of Kitzbühel. Local trains stop at Hahnenkamm Station which lies closer to the town centre than Kitzbühel Station. On a scorching hot afternoon in 1991 we alighted at Kitzbühel with luggage having travelled from Kärnten. We knew the name of our hotel but not its precise location. It turned out to be adjacent to Hahnenkamm station but we only discovered that after struggling with the luggage uphill through the town centre and out the other side. Had we known, we could simply have waited at Kitzbühel for the next local train and travelled round the loop to the next stop at Hahnenkamm.

Having turned direction, trains for Salzburg face slightly west of north in Kitzbühel Station. The Hahnenkamm is behind on the left and the Kitzbühelerhorn to the right. Both can be reached by cable car.

The Wilder Kaiser, a range of mountains looking like enormous teeth dominate the middle distance to the north west as the train approaches St Johann in Tirol. From here you can get a bus to Ellman, the lower station of the Hartkaiserbahn funicular.

There used to be a funicular at St Johann itself climbing southwards to Angereralm but this was replaced by a cable car during the 1980s.

The railway continues southeast from St Johann and begins to climb up the valley of the Pillersee Ache towards the summit of the line at Hochfilzen which marks the border between the Tirol and Salzburgerland.

Sporting an experimental livery, 1044.210 arrives at Kirchberg with the Inter City 'Wilder Kaiser', the 12.40 from Wien West on 20 August 1993. The signal box is Kirchberg Stellwerke 1.   *(Martin Bairstow)*

Two storey station building at Hopfgarten looking towards Kirchberg in 1991.
(Martin Bairstow)

The smaller station at Brixen im Thale. The 'Fahrdienstleiter' sits in the front office on the left. He emerges onto the platform with red hat whenever a train calls or passes through. His office has a ticket window inside the waiting room.
(Philippa Simpson)

Descending through the Griessenpass then continuing above the Leoganger Valley, the scene becomes more pastoral. The valley opens out as the line curves southwards.

There are extensive sidings at Saalfelden which is served by 'Inter City' trains. The mountain section is now over and speed increases. The railway skirts the shore of Zellersee. Half way along is the town of Zell am See where a narrow gauge train begins its hour and a half journey through the Oberpinzgau to Krimml.

The main line turns east into the Unterpinzgau. At this point immediately south of Zellersee, the valley is very wide but as the railway follows the River Salzach it encounters a number of narrow gorges. Although the Salzach provided an obvious route all the way to Salzburg, it was not necessarily an easy one and a number of tunnels were necessary where the rock face encroaches upon the river itself leaving no space for the railway. At certain points the east and westbound lines part company briefly because there was insufficient room when the second track was laid in 1912-15 causing it to resort to more tunnelling than had been necessary on the first occasion.

Just beyond Lend, the Tauern Line comes visible on the hillside, gradually descending to meet the Giselabahn at the entrance to the station at Schwarzach – St Veit.

Passenger services on the Giselabahn comprise both Inter City and local trains every hour. Alternate loco hauled expresses run between Innsbruck and Wien Westbahnhof via Salzburg, alternating with Trans Alpin sets from Innsbruck to Graz. The two services part company at Bischofshofen, 14km north of Schwarzach – St Veit. The local trains, all stations from Wörgl to Salzburg, are mainly class 4130 three coach emus but there are a few loco hauled workings, mainly those hauling additional vans.

A Class 1044 arrives at Schwarzsee Halt with a local for Wörgl in June 1991, the first month of 'Neue Austro Takt' which brought this local service up to hourly, about double the previous erratic interval.

(Martin Bairstow)

1042.044 in the old green livery pauses at Hahnenkamm with a Salzburg to Wörgl local in June 1991. The signalman cum booking clerk sits behind the bay window to the left of the locomotive.

(Martin Bairstow)

Hahnenkamm Station June 1991. Pub/cafeteria to the right of the booking hall. Ticket office in the 'Fahrdienstraum' to the left. *(Martin Bairstow)*

The main station building at Kitzbühel in January 1992. The snow has been cleared for the buses which, as so often in Austria, terminate at the railway station.
(Martin Bairstow)

The remote station at Leogang (840 metres above sea level) on a bleak day in June 1991.
(Martin Bairstow)

1010.11 calls at Zell am See with an eastbound express in August 1984. At that time, each track was served by a narrow low platform to which access was gained by one of the sleeper crossings. This was a typical arrangement until recent times. *(Martin Bairstow)*

Zell am See looking south on 25 August 1993 with 4030.302 on the 11.13 Salzburg to Wörgl stopping service. *(Martin Bairstow)*

Modernisation has swept away Zell am See Stellwerke 2 which used to operate the points and level crossing at the north end of the station, seen here in August 1984. *(Martin Bairstow)*

The 'steamer' service on Zellersee comprises an Überfahrt to Bellevue and Kurpark and a Rundfahrt which involves a 40 minute circuit of the lake non landing. The 'Kitzsteinhorn' sets out on such a mission on 25 August 1993   *(Martin Bairstow)*

View eastward from a train stopped at Kitzlochklamm Halt. The two tracks keep parting company. They were built at different times and had to take slightly different alignments through the gorge.
(Martin Bairstow)

With driving trailer 6010.009 leading, the eastbound 'Schöckl', the 9.20 Innsbruck to Graz leaves Zell am See on 25 August 1993. *(Martin Bairstow)*

A class 1044 passing Eschenau Station, unstaffed and unmodernised, with the Inter City 'Tirolerland' from Wörgl to Wien West on 25 August 1993. *(Martin Bairstow)*

The 'Trans Alpin' units

The class 4010 'Trans Alpin' set really is a magnificent train. There are 29 sets built between 1965 and 1978. Each comprises a streamlined locomotive with luggage space followed by an open second, a corridor second, a restaurant/buffet, a corridor composite and finally an open first with a streamlined driving end identical in appearance to the front of the locomotive.

Total seating is only 162 second class and 66 first plus 42 unclassified in the catering vehicle. (There are variations in the restaurant/buffet vehicles between different sets). The reason for the comparatively low capacity is the spacious accommodation. The open second, towards which I always make a bee line, has 2 + 1 seating. Even today it compares well with anything else running on the ÖBB but remember that, in 1965, upholstered seating was a rarity on the Continent.

When I stayed at St Anton in 1976, the 'Trans Alpins' were the only trains which offered soft seating. This was at a time when we took BR mark 1 and 2 comfort for granted but the 'Trans Alpins' were and still are much more spacious which is great most of the time.

They are of course rather less fun when crowded. Higher capacity vehicles might at least provide a seat for everybody. But we did learn the secret when leaving Innsbruck by the 17.20 'Grimming'. We were travelling in August 1993 from St Anton to Kirchberg and had changed at Innsbruck off the Euro City 'Maria Theresia' with no time to spare. The 'Trans Alpin' set working the 'Grimming' was already full with commuters so we took our seats in the buffet car, ordered a cup of tea and made it last the hour to Kirchberg. We were not the only people to do this. Subsequent observation showed that some commuters were doing it every day.

Philippa lets the train take the strain. On board the Inter City 'Schöckl', somewhere between Zell am See and Kitzbühel on 18 January 1992. The open second accommodates 60 passengers with 2 + 1 seating.
(Martin Bairstow)

Evening rush hour on the 17.20 out of Innsbruck. Sporting a Settle-Carlisle sweatshirt, Philippa has come to a temporary stand alongside the Achenseebahn carriage siding in Jenbach platform. Can she make that cup of tea last till Kirchberg?
(Martin Bairstow)

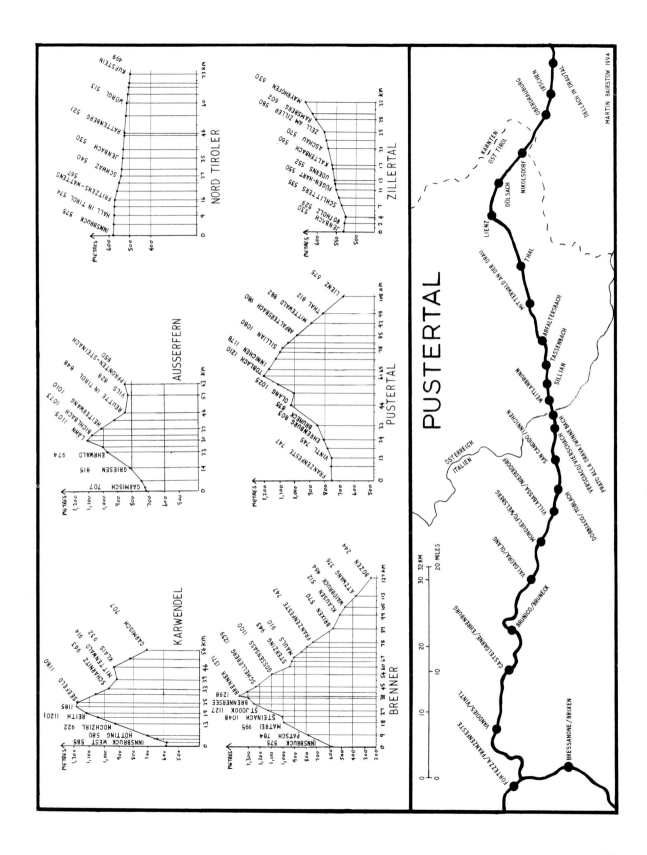

The Pinzgau Bahn

Zell am See – Krimml

The main line 'Giselabahn' has followed the River Salzach all the way from Salzburg but at Zell am See it swings north and takes to the mountains. If you wish to travel any further up the valley, then you change trains at Zell am See onto the 76cm gauge Pinzgaubahn which runs for 54km as far as Krimml. Dating from 1898, the line is part of the ÖBB. The Pinzgau refers to the upper valley of the Salzach, all the way from Lend to the waterfalls at Krimml.

The line begins in two bay platforms at the south end of Zell am See Station and runs parallel with the main line for a short distance to the first halt at Tischlerhäusl where the shed is situated. The first 7km as far as Bruckberg Golfplatz Halt enjoys an intensive service – almost half hourly. This facility was introduced after delivery of the line's five class 5090 diesel railcars in 1986. Over the remainder of the line there are nine return workings daily taking just over 1½ hours for the through journey.

Passenger trains may comprise a railcar with or without a trailer, or maybe loco hauled with or without a special van for bicycles. The departure sheets at stations carry symbols to distinguish the bicycle facility for each train. 'Sehr gut geeignet'

means it conveys a bicycle van; 'beshränkt geeignet' means it has an ordinary van whilst 'Beförderung nicht möglich' denotes no van at all so no bicycles can be accommodated.

A special steam service operates on Tuesdays and Thursdays in July and August and on Saturdays in September, leaving Zell am See at 9.30. Return departure is at 15.48 from Krimml. The journey takes 2½ hours each way. Motive power is 0-8-4 No 399.001, built for the St Pölten to Mariazell line in 1906.

Standing on a plinth at Mittersill Station is 0-6-2T No 298.55 which was built for the opening of the Pinzgaubahn in 1898.

The main goods traffic on the Krimml line appears to be straw. On 4 August 1993, 29 loaded transporter wagons were noted at various locations on the line (Austrian Railway Group Journal No 8). Most carried straw but a few appeared to have standard gauge aggregate wagons on board.

Travellers looking for an alternative to covering the Pinzgau line in both directions may effect a circular tour by using the bus over the Gerlos Pass from Krimml to either Zell am Ziller or Mayrhofen on the Zillertalbahn.

2095.002 waits departure from Zell am See for Krimml on 10 June 1991. The station has been substantially rebuilt since the 1984 view on page 31 (top). *(Martin Bairstow)*

Steam in Pinzgau. 0-8-4 No. 399.01 with a short special travelling west near Hollersbach Halt on 23 August 1987. *(John Holroyd)*

(This page)

Right 5090.003 calls at Zellermoos Halt with the 13.37 Krimml to Zell am See on 25 August 1993. This section of the route enjoys a fairly intensive commuter service.
(Martin Bairstow)

Middle The well kept station at Niedernsill, August 1993.
(Martin Bairstow)

Lower The equally tidy halt at Lengdorf. 5090.003 enters with a trailer on the 13.37 ex Krimml on 25 August 1993.
(Martin Bairstow)

CENTRE PAGE PHOTOS

Top left The 'Giselabahn' follows the River Salzach all the way from Salzburg to Zell am See. 1044.076 is in charge of a westbound freight approaching Eschenau in Lower Pinzgau on 25 August 1993.
(Martin Bairstow)

Bottom left 1044.220 with a train of German Inter City stock at Seefeld in Tirol working the 'Karwendel', the prestige train of the day over this route, through from Dortmund to Innsbruck.
(Martin Bairstow)

Top right Steam in Pustertal July 1974. A class 741 'Franco Crosti' 2-8-0 pauses at Bruneck with an eastbound service. Facilities for loading parcels appear as vintage as the train itself.
(Iain Parsons)

Bottom right Stubaitalbahn No 2, built 1904, deposits a passenger at Nockhofweg Halt on the climb up to Fulpmes on 16 August 1970. The line was modernised in 1983 but No 2 was converted to run on d.c. and can still be seen on special workings. *(Douglas Butterfield)*

Die Zugfuhrerin (lady guard) gives the right away from the tiny halt of Walchen in Pinzgau bound for Krimml on 25 August 1993. *(Martin Bairstow)*

0-6-2T No 298.55 stands on a plinth of Mittersill Station to remind us of the original 1898 motive power on the Pinzgaubahn. *(John Holroyd)*

2095.15 on arrival at Krimml in August 1984. At that time I wondered about the future of this line but it has since acquired some new rolling stock and a better service *(Martin Bairstow)*

The Arlberg Route

Innsbruck – Landeck – Bludenz

The main line west from Innsbruck follows the Inn Valley for the first 75km as far as Landeck. There the mountain section begins and, in the next 63km, the line climbs at a maximum of 1 in 38 to St Anton where it enters the Arlberg Tunnel 10.25km (just under 6½ miles) in length. Emerging at Langen in the Province of Vorarlberg, the line begins an even steeper descent at up to 1 in 32 to reach Bludenz, which at 560 metres above sea level is actually a bit lower than Innsbruck.

Beyond Bludenz, the railway continues to Feldkirch where a 'branch' diverges into Switzerland passing through the independent principality of Liechtenstein. The Austrian main line continues north from Feldkirch to Bregenz, the capital of Vorarlberg, which stands on Bodensee (Lake Constance).

The Arlberg Route is the only rail link between Vorarlberg and the rest of Austria. Prior to its completion in 1884, communication with Vorarlberg was dependent either on road transport over the Arlberg Pass or, more practically, on rail transit via Bavaria. The latter option worked very well in normal times, but there was a war between Austria and Germany in 1865/6 and a further conflict between France and Germany in 1870/1 which rendered Vorarlberg virtually isolated, hungry and easy prey to foreign aggression. The Arlberg Railway was thus of both strategic and commercial importance.

Legislation authorising the project was signed by the Emperor on 7 May 1880 after at least 15 years of debate as to the best route. Alternatives which were rejected included a route further south using the Paznaun and Montafon Valleys and a route involving an Arlberg Tunnel only half the length of the one actually built but with steeper ascents on either side.

Work on the Arlberg Tunnel began at the St Anton end on 14 June 1880 and at Langen a week later. The two sides met on 13 November 1883. By that time, the relatively easy section of route from Innsbruck to Landeck had opened on 1 July 1883. This assisted progress on the mountain section by allowing materials to be brought nearer to site by rail.

The first test train travelled through the Arlberg on 3 September 1884. Freight traffic began three days later. The official opening was carried out in the presence of the Emperor on 20 September with public passenger trains beginning the next day.

The Arlberg Tunnel was built double track but the rest of the line was single and remained so until comparatively recent times. There was a terrible smoke problem in the tunnel. Electrification was discussed as early as the 1890s but technology was not sufficiently advanced at that stage. The Simplon became the first of the great Alpine Tunnels to be electrified from its opening in 1906.

Electric trains reached Landeck from Innsbruck at the end of 1923. Electric working through the Arlberg Tunnel began on 20 November 1924. The Landeck to St Anton and Langen to Bludenz sections followed during the first half of 1925. Within two years, the programme of electrification in Western Austria was complete with the conversion of the route beyond Bludenz to Bregenz and to Buchs (SG) in Switzerland.

Trains for the Arlberg Route leave Innsbruck Hauptbahnhof facing south but, after passing under the Olympiabrücke, they part company with the Brenner Line and turn right through 90% on the Konzertkurve which leads into the Westbahnhof. This station was known as Wilton prior to 1907 when the Hauptbahnhof was also renamed from being the Südbahnhof.

The line leaves Innsbruck Westbahnhof under the shadow of the elevated motorway section which forms the approach to the Brenner Autobahn. The single track Karwendelbahn branches off on the right. Over the next few kilometres this can be seen weaving its way in and out of tunnels on the mountainside on the far side of the valley as it makes its steep climb towards Seefeld.

Double track was achieved from Innsbruck as far as Zirl in 1969 and continued to Telfs – Pfaffenhofen in 1977. This made possible the improvement in local service over this section in 1979 using then new class 4020 electric units. Ötztal, 47km from Innsbruck, was reached in 1987 allowing the extension of some local trains.

The 122 metre Ötztaler Ache Brücke is the first of a number of major bridges and viaducts on the route. It is the third bridge at this site having been replaced during the 1920s and again in 1968.

The Inn Valley now begins to close in with the railway running alongside the river whose bank has had to be reinforced in places. Soon after the village of Roppen, the Inntal turns into a narrow ravine with just sufficient room for the railway on the southern bank. On the approach to Imst – Pitztal, the River Pitze joins the Inn requiring another substantial bridge.

The station at Imst – Pitztal is built on a small area of flat land created by a bend in the river. The valley is now a bit wider but with sheer cliffs on both sides. The railway remains on the south side of the Inn as far as Landeck.

Double track is being extended the 27km from Ötztal to Landeck. The work, sections of which should be completed by 1997, involves a lot of new alignment which will give passengers a faster ride but with some of the most interesting sections bypassed in new tunnels.

Leaving Ötztal, the line will swing away from the river with a 200 metre Wassertaltunnel and a new bridge over the Ötztaler Ache. Roppen Station will be in the same place but, soon after, the line will cross to the north bank of the Inn and enter the

1042.615 approaching Landeck-Perfuchs Halt on the descent from the Arlberg with the 4.07am Bregenz-Wien West on 21 July 1982.

(Mike Parsons)

1044.13 brings the 6.54 Lindau to Innsbruck across the Innbrücke into Landeck on 21 July 1982. *(Mike Parsons)*

Inter City 'Montfort', the 14.17 Bregenz to Wien Westbahnhof passing Pians on 5 July 1992. *(David Beeken)*

Strengen looking towards St Anton on 6 July 1969. The station stands at the bottom of the narrow valley. *(Geoffrey Lewthwaite)*

Driving trailer 6010.01 bringing up the rear of two 'Trans Alpin' sets forming the 'Trans Alpin' service from Basel to Wien Westbahnhof in July 1976. It is seen descending from St Anton towards St Jakob. In those days, the 'Trans Alpin' sets were the only trains with upholstered seats in both first and second class. There was compulsory seat reservation for the Swiss section of this prestige train.
(Martin Bairstow)

Modern motive power on the rather sparse Arlberg local service 4020.112 waits its next turn of duty on 26 August 1993. *(Martin Bairstow)*

A class 1020 in charge of a westbound freight passing St Anton in July 1976.
(Martin Bairstow)

2,825 metre Karrer Tunnel. The steep cliffs before Imst – Pitztal will be pierced by two tunnels, the Waldeler (255 metres) and Osternstein (790 metres) between which the line will emerge briefly to cross the Pitztaler Ache on a new bridge.

Beyond Imsterberg, the route will follow a new path, mostly in tunnel, for 7km. Imsterbergtunnel (3,500 metres) will lead to a resited Schönwies Station beyond which will be Maiswaldtunnel (1,550 metres). After a short stretch utilising the existing alignment, the line will plunge into a new Zammertunnel (3,600 metres) leading direct into Landeck Station.

Landeck marks the end of the Inn Valley section of the route and the beginning of serious climbing. The Inn is crossed by a bridge 195 metres in length. Climbing at an average of 1 in 43, the line soon finds itself on a ledge high above the Rosanna.

Beyond Pians, the Wiesberg Castle comes into view perched precariously by the lineside above the valley. Below is the confluence of the Rivers Rosanna and Trisanna which heralds the Trisanna Brücke. This carries the railway 86 metres above the Trisanna on a central span, 119 metres in length. The original Trisanna Brücke was similar in appearance to the present one but with more beams and cross members. It was strengthened at electrification with the addition of a 'fish belly' but was completely replaced in 1964 with only minimal interruption to traffic.

Originally, the line used to turn sharply to the right after leaving the bridge and follow the Stanzertal with a couple of short tunnels. But due to repeated blockages by landslides this section was replaced just prior to the First World War by an alignment further to the south involving the short Weinzeirltunnel which emerges briefly onto the old alignment before heading into the 1643 metre Moltertobeltunnel.

The three track station at Strengen occupies every bit of available space on the southern side of the steep sloped valley. The single track hugs the contours as it negotiates the Stanzertal Gorge. Then beyond Flirsch, the valley opens out to reveal an Alpine basin in which are located the tourist villages of Pettneu and St Anton.

It is only intended to double parts of the mountain section between Landeck and Bludenz. The first stretch to be converted will be the relatively easy 9km between Schann and St Anton. This, combined with the Arlbergtunnel itself, will give a 20km length of double track.

The ten minute journey through the Arlberg takes us from the Tirol into Vorarlberg. It marks the watershed between the Rosanna which flows east via the Inn and the Danube into the Black Sea and the Alfenz which flows west via the Rhine into the North Sea. On many days it can also signal a change in the weather.

1670.22 (wheel arrangement 1A BO A1 which is roughly 2-8-2), stands at St Anton Am Arlberg in July 1976 having brought a local train of 4 wheel carriages in from Landeck. The class 1670 dating from 1928 is now withdrawn though some examples are preserved.

(Martin Bairstow)

Langen Station stands high on the north side of the Klöstertal. For the next 25kms the line falls at an average of 1 in 38 but with long sections at 1 in 30 until it reaches the valley floor.

The train enters Klösterle station by the Wäldlitobelbrücke which crosses the stream rushing down from the Spullersee Reservoir high above the valley. The ÖBB have harnessed the 800 metre high head of water to build their own power station at Wald.

Between Klösterle and Wald stations, there are three avalanche shelters, together nearly a km in length. The 505 metre Grosstobeltunnel was opened in 1892 after the original route had been lost in a landslide. 20 years later, a similar thing happened causing the 1157 metre Wildentobeltunnel to be built.

The station building at Dalaas is of more modern appearance than others on the line. The original was demolished and ten of its occupants killed on 11 January 1954 when an avalanche threw 1020.42 against it. The locomotive had been stranded there with a passenger train since the previous day.

In the next 4km to Hintergasse, the line burrows in and out of the mountainside no fewer than five times in short tunnels, none over 250 metres in length.

The Schmiedtobel Viaduct, 52 metres high, carries the train between the tunnels which penetrate the Eigelwand Cliff. This and many other features can best be observed from the valley floor.

The last of the tunnels on this section, the 78 metre Funffingertobel leads into Hintergrasse station which is built entirely on a viaduct except for the bit adjacent to the station building. Anyone wishing to catch a train here must climb a long, steep, twisting footpath from the valley below. There are however only a handful of stopping trains.

Schanatobelbrücke below Hintegrasse was built in 1968 after its predecessor had been carried by an avalanche 200 metres down the valley.

Long sweeping curves, first to the left then to the right bring the line into Braz. The line no longer clings to the mountainside but the gradient continues, easing to 1 in 50 after Bings, until 1km from Bludenz the descent from the Arlberg is complete. The Montafonerbahn joins on the left and there is double track for the last bit into Bludenz where, in 1993, the station was undergoing rebuilding with more substantial platforms, subways etc.

The principal passenger service over the Arlberg route is the two hourly 'Inter City' from Bregenz to Wien Westbahnhof. Between Bludenz and Innsbruck this serves Langen, St Anton, Landeck, Imst – Pitztal, Ötztal and Tels – Pfaffenhofen. Departures from Bludenz are from 5.00 until 21.00, the last two not going all the way to Wien.

The 'Euro Cities' also assume a regular interval pattern during the daytime with departures from Bludenz at:

9.27	'Franz Schubert'	Zürich - Wien
11.27	'Transalpin'	Basel - Wien
13.25	'Robert Stolz'	Zürich - Graz
15.27	'Maria Theresia'	Zürich - Wien
17.59	'Wiener Symphoniker'	Bregenz - Wien

The last named is a 'Super City' which actually offers the fastest journey of the day from Bregenz to Wien in 7 hours 40 minutes for 708km which is quite commendable given the mountainous terrain. Whether the 00.58 arrival in Wien strikes a chord with many customers is perhaps another question.

Local services over the mountain section of the Arlberg route are quite sparse. There are only three such trains serving intermediate stations between St Anton and Landeck.

The service east of Landeck is better with trains (almost) every two hours. Then it is (almost) hourly from Ötztal with additional trains Mondays to Fridays providing a more intensive service from Telfs – Pfaffenhofen into Innsbruck.

A mixed freight disappears into the east portal of the 6$\frac{1}{2}$ mile long Arlberg Tunnel in July 1976.   *(Martin Bairstow)*

A class 1044 restarts from Langen and crosses the Alfenzbrücke prior to entering the Arlberg Tunnel with the 8.43 Bregenz to Wien West 'Bodensee' on 27 June 1983.

(Mike Parsons)

The 21.45 overnight express from Wien West to Bregenz has almost completed its descent of the Arlberg as it approaches Braz on 27 July 1976. The formation includes a sleeping car.

(Martin Bairstow)

Vintage Electrics

The decision to electrify all the main lines in Western Austria was taken in 1920. The Alpine routes were obvious candidates for electrification because of the gradients, the availability of hydro electricity and the cost of importing coal, Austria having lost its domestic source with the independence of Czechoslovakia.

Some of the electric locomotives, built in the 1920s have enjoyed longevity though 1993 did see the end of some classes after more than 60 years service. Amongst the casualties was D(0-8-0) No. 1061-002, the last of a class dating from 1926 which had finished its days shunting at Innsbruck. Also extinct during the year were the remaining E(0-10-0)s of class 1080 and 1180 dating from 1924-27. The last 1180s had been based at Bludenz and Landeck.

The ÖBB still has three class 1045 Bo-Bos, built 1927-28, one of which is going to be preserved but two of this class have already been sold for further service on the Montafonerbahn.

There are still three class 1145s (built 1927-31) working local freight from Innsbruck and Wörgl but the main attention of connoisseurs is now directed at the dwindling number of class 1020 Co-Cos.

These were built between 1940 and 1944 for the Deutsche Reichsbahn. The ÖBB was allocated 44 of them after the war and actually built three more itself in 1954. A larger number ended up on the DB which has retained two for special traffic. The others went to East Germany where they remained in use until the partial collapse of freight traffic after unification in 1990.

The Austrian fleet is now in decline but was still evident in 1993 on freight duties and banking heavy passenger trains over the Arlberg.

1020.012 with heavy freight at Jenbach in June 1991. The train is waiting to be overtaken by a passenger train.
(Martin Bairstow)

1145.14 prepares to assist a German loco on the climb from Innsbruck to Brenner in August 1973   *(Stuart Baker)*

The Montafoner Bahn

Bludenz – Schruns

Schruns Station looking towards Bludenz on August 1993. The train is a two coach unit either ET 10.103 or 104 with its driving trailer nearest the camera.
(Martin Bairstow)

Had the Arlberg Route taken a more southerly course as was once mooted, then the Montafon Valley would have acquired a railway earlier than 1905. As it was, it had to wait for 21 years after completion of the Arlberg Line. During this time, there was discussion of a metre gauge line but when the 12.7km branch finally opened between Bludenz and Schruns on 18 December 1905, it had the distinction of being the first standard gauge electric line in the Austrian Empire.

The system of electrification was 800 volts d.c. fed from an overhead wire. When the Arlberg Route was being electrified in 1925, the d.c. overhead had to be removed between Bludenz Station and the junction. For a short time, Montafonerbahn trains had to be steam hauled under the a.c. wires but later on they were equipped with batteries.

The branch had been operated since opening by the Austrian State Railways but in 1926 it was transferred to the independent Montafonerbahn A.G. Freight traffic blossomed with the building of a power station at Partenen further up the Montafon Valley. This was reached by a 76cm gauge line from Tschagguns Station, 18km in length. Standard gauge wagons were conveyed right through to

Partenen on transporters. A limited passenger service operated on the narrow gauge line which closed in 1953.

The Montafonerbahn was converted to the main line a.c. electrification on 6 March 1972 permitting normal running into Bludenz. Old rolling stock was either converted, scrapped or, in the case of centre cab loco No 10.002, sold to Stern & Hafferl for use on their Vorchdorf to Eggenberg line.

Since 1972, the Montafonerbahn has acquired a variety of second hand rolling stock including two ÖBB locomotives 1045.01 and 1045.03 dating from 1927. In 1990 the line took delivery from the ÖBB of one of the original class 4130 'Trans Alpin' sets now renumbered 10.105. The following year, the Montafonerbahn purchased a brand new two car set No 10.107 which was built as an add on to a larger order for the Swiss Federal Railways.

For steam specials, the Montafonerbahn retains 0-8-0T No 178.84, which was built in Linz in 1909 together with four vintage 4 wheel carriages.

Leaving Bludenz station, which is currently being rebuilt, the train for Schruns runs parallel with the Arlberg line for 1.5km before striking off in a southerly direction just before Bludenz – Moos halt. The line begins to climb at 1 in 60. It crosses the

ET 10.104 at Bludenz in 1983, long before work began to reconstruct the station with raised platforms, subways etc. The railcar started life in 1935 as a German diesel vehicle (DB No VT 63907). It was rebuilt at Schruns in 1974. Sister vehicle ET 10.103 (VT 63905) had preceded it in 1965 when the Montafonerbahn rebuilt it as a dual voltage unit.

(Mike Parsons)

Latest Swiss technology on the Montafonerbahn. ET 10.107 at Bludenz where the new platforms are emerging on August 1993. *(Martin Bairstow)*

The new train certainly affords adequate comfort for a journey of 20 minutes.

(Martin Bairstow)

River Alfenz by a steel bridge just before the cement works at Lorüns which is the Montafonerbahn's biggest freight customer. The valley becomes much narrower. There are two crossings of the River III before the line reaches its steepest section at 1 in 40. The valley begins to open out beyond St Anton in Montafon. The railway workshops are situated at Schruns which at 681 metres above sea level is 120 metres higher than Bludenz.

The passenger timetable shows 22 return trips in the day. It is not a perfect 'Taktfahrplan' but there is a train virtually every hour with a 30 minute interval during the morning and evening peaks. The journey takes 20 minutes.

A Lost Opportunity

The Reschenbahn Project

Besides the Brenner, there is one other point where the mountain range between Nord and Südtirol drops to 1,500 metres. This is at the Reschenpass, close to the border with Switzerland.

In 1908, a standard gauge line was projected from Landeck up the Inn Valley as far as Pfunds. From here the Inn Valley continues into Switzerland and it was hoped that a metre gauge connection would be built to join the Rhätische Bahn at Scuol-Tarasp.

From Pfunds, the standard gauge was projected to climb at a maximum of 1 in 40 over the Reschenpass to Mals in Südtirol from where an existing line continued down the Etsch Valley to Meran and eventually to Bozen.

Being so far west, the route would never have been able to compete with the Brenner Line. Only preliminary work was done before the First World War brought things to a halt.

Then in 1918, the military decided that they needed an alternative to the Brenner and so work started using Russian prisoners of war. Some progress was achieved including a 1,250 metre tunnel at Landeck but work stopped again when the war ended.

In 1925, Austria asked Italy, as new landlords of the Südtirol, if they would like to make a financial contribution towards the work already accomplished. That was enough to put the project permanently on ice.

During the latter part of the Second World War, the Germans, who controlled both Austria and Northern Italy, decided that they could use an alternative to the Brenner. Work resumed again on the Reschen project only to stop when the war ended.

The partially completed works were mainly on the Nordtirol side. Ownership passed to the ÖBB but in 1954 the decision was made to sell these off.

Destined always to remain a terminus. Scuol-Tarasp looking north east along the Inn Valley towards Austria. Rhätische Bahn Bo-Bo No 617 'Ilanz' runs round after bringing in a train from St Moritz on 29 May 1979.

(Martin Bairstow)

The Karwendel Bahn

Innsbruck – Seefeld – Garmisch-Partenkirchen

1042.612 arrives at Seefeld in Tirol with a local from Mittenwald to Innsbruck on 22 August 1993.
(Martin Bairstow)

Readers familiar with Swiss Railways should know what I mean if I liken the climb from Innsbruck up to Seefeld with that of the Bern Lötschberg Simplon Railway out of the Rhone Valley from Brig towards the Lötschberg Tunnel.

Leaving the Arlberg Route at Innsbruck Westbahnhof, the single track crosses the River Inn then calls at Hötting Station leaving which the climb begins. The maximum gradient is 1 in 27, the average is steeper than 1 in 35 as the line climbs from 580 metres at Hötting to 1,185 metres at the summit just short of Seefeld Station.

There are no fewer than 16 tunnels in the 21km between Hötting and the summit with a combined length of nearly 4.5 km. The longest is the Martinswand Tunnel at 1,810 metres between Kranebitten and Hochzirl. When the line is not in tunnel, it runs on a ledge on the mountainside affording a view over the Inn Valley below. Conversely, the Seefeld line can be viewed from a train on the Arlberg Route all the way to Inzing. There are 12 major bridges and viaducts over the various ravines and side valleys.

Once over the summit, the line drops fairly gently to Seefeld Station. Seefeld is a very popular holiday resort for both Winter and Summer seasons. We enjoyed a week there in March 1992.

Innsbruck Airport is very close. Although Seefeld is anything but central to the ÖBB network, it would be possible to get four days value out of a 'Rabbit Card' from a base there. We did something a little different and had a five day Bavarian Regional Rover on the DB paying day return to Scharnitz Grenze (frontier) each time we ventured out of Austria.

From Seefeld to Scharnitz, the descent is steeper than 1 in 40. A little way beyond Scharnitz Station the line passes into Germany. The descent continues to Mittenwald but there is then a slight rise to Klais which at 932 metres above sea level proclaims itself as the highest 'Inter City' station in Germany. The descent is then resumed. Another 10km at an average steeper than 1 in 40 brings us to Garmisch-Partenkirchen.

The Karwendelbahn, or Mittenwaldbahn, was built under an agreement of 1904 between Austria and Germany. A proportion of the cost came, on the Austrian side, from the Imperial Government, from the Province of Tirol and the City of Innsbruck.

The bold decision was taken to electrify the line at 15,000 volts a.c. using the then pioneer system which was to become the standard in Austria, Germany and Switzerland.

Steam operation began between Garmisch-

Partenkirchen and Scharnitz on 1 July 1912. A few months later, the Austrian section opened with electric traction between Innsbruck and Mittenwald. Nine C1 (0-6-2) locomotives were provided of class 1060. They had a maximum speed of 40 km per hour which must compare well to what steam could have achieved on those gradients. More important than the top speed would be the consistent performance of the electrics compared with steam. When the route from Mittenwald to Garmisch-Partenkirchen became available for electric traction in April 1913, these Austrian locos had to work the through service alone. By the end of 1913, the Imperial Bavarian Railways had five 1C1 (2-6-2)

locos available which took their turn in running through to Innsbruck. This practice has continued ever since with interworking of ÖBB and DB locos and rolling stock.

Trains nowadays leave Innsbruck for Mittenwald approximately every hour but it is by no means a precise 'Taktfahrplan'. Of the 14 daily departures, three are 'Korridorzüge' through to Reutte in Tirol (see next chapter), one is the Inter City 'Karwendel' to Dortmund, two others are through to München and the remainder are just locals to Mittenwald, mostly with connections to Garmisch-Partenkirchen and beyond.

The 13.06 Mittenwald to Innsbruck formed by a class 4020 unit calls at Hötting on 22 August 1993. Our northbound local waits for the signal to commence the steep ascent of the Karwendelbahn.
(Martin Bairstow)

Two or three passengers alight at Reith from the morning München–Innsbruck semi fast on 24 March 1992.
(Martin Bairstow)

Three car electric unit 4020 120 (built 1987) at Seefeld travelling towards Mittenwald. The view is northwards. *(Martin Bairstow)*

Giessenbach Halt looking towards Scharnitz in March 1992. *(Martin Bairstow)*

Scharnitz, frontier station and passing loop, March 1992. We have waited for DB103.308 to clear the section from Seefeld with an Innsbruck to München working. *(Martin Bairstow)*

Mittenwald looking north in March 1992. ÖBB4020.120 has arrived from Innsbruck. DB113.266 prepares to leave for the Tirolean capital. Passengers for Austria are directed to this end of the platform via a deserted customs hall in the station building. Rakes of German passenger stock fill the sidings as some long distance trains terminate here from the north. *(Martin Bairstow)*

A regular visitor to the Karwendel Line is 'Der Gläsernenzug' (the glass train) which operates a programme of excursions from its base in München. 491.001 was built in 1935. It is seen at Klais, 'the Highest Inter City Station in Germany' travelling towards Innsbruck in March 1992. The view is looking west.

(Martin Bairstow)

The Ausserfern Bahn

Garmisch-Partenkirchen – Reutte in Tirol

Reutte in Tirol looking north on 27 March 1992. The German dmu No 628.020 is the 16.28 to Kempten. 113.266 affords more than adequate power for the single coach 16.58 to Garmisch-Partenkirchen.

(Martin Bairstow)

Situated in the extreme north of the Tirol, Reutte stands on the River Lech. This flows from the Arlberg north-eastwards into Germany.

The building of a railway north from Reutte was a comparatively easy business. The line which, opened on 16 December 1905, follows the Lech Valley on a falling gradient as far as Ulrichsbrücke – Füssen at which point the Lech turns north east, crosses the border into Germany and flows into Forggensee. The railway continues northwest up the tributary valley of the River Vils to cross the border just beyond Schönbichl. The line then continues on German territory through Pfronten – Steinach and on to Kempten.

When the route opened, it was operated exclusively by the Bavarian Railways whose successor, the DB now provides a dmu service at roughly two hourly intervals between Reutte and Kempten.

Communication between Reutte and the rest of Austria was somewhat more difficult. The obvious route lay through the Ausserfern as far as Ehrwald but a direct progression from there to Innsbruck was blocked by the Mieminger Gebirge which rise to over 2,500 metres.

In 1910, Austria and Germany agreed to build the Ausserfernbahn from Reutte via Ehrwald then northwards towards Garmisch-Partenkirchen where connection would be made with the Karwendelbahn, then under construction.

The line opened on 29 May 1913. It was electrified from the outset at 15,000 volts d.c. Until September 1993, the majority of trains were worked by DB locomotives but there were three trains per day through from Innsbruck to Reutte in Tirol at 7.40, 15.06 and 18.27 worked by ÖBB stock. These take just under 2½ hours for the through journey and have at least one carriage reserved as a 'Korridorwagen' for passengers travelling through between the two parts of Austria. They are not supposed to join or alight at stops between Scharnitz and Ehrwald in return for which they are spared passport and customs control.

Return departures from Reutte are at 5.52, 12.09 and 18.25 through to Innsbruck. There are other services between Reutte and Garmisch-Partenkirchen.

The line climbs at a maximum of 1 in 27 from Reutte towards the Klausen Tunnel (512.5 metres) through which the line curves to face in a south easterly direction. The summit of 1,105 metres is reached at Lähn after which the descent begins at 1 in 33 through the Lichtenberg Valley. There are two concrete viaducts, the first of five arches then beyond Lermoos station another of four.

The descent continues as the line turns into a northerly direction through Ehrwald. The valley of the River Loisach leads across the German border to the closed station at Griesen where the German border police may be waiting to board if they have nothing else to do. All the stations are closed between the border and Garmisch-Partenkirchen. For the final 3 km into Garmisch, the metre gauge Bayerische Zugspitzbahn runs alongside. This is a mountain rack line which reaches the 2,968 metre summit of the Zugspitze which lies right on the border between Germany and Austria. The journey to the summit takes an hour and involves a change at Grainau where the rack section begins. The final assault of the Zugspitze is in tunnel.

In 1993, it was decided that the cost of renewing the electrical equipment on the lightly used Ausserfernbahn could not be justified. So after 80 years electric operation, it is to change to diesel, probably with newly built dmus of Class 5147. Hopefully these may provide a lease of life to a line which has been threatened from time to time. There is certainly scope for a more efficient operation of this service in terms of both rolling stock utilisation and manpower.

The tiny station building at Lähn, March 1992.
(Martin Bairstow)

The loco shed at the north end of Reutte in Tirol Station.
(Martin Bairstow)

The Rosshütte Bahn

Opened in 1969, this 120cm gauge funicular begins on the east side of Seefeld, about 1km uphill from the ÖBB station. 2.5km in length, the line rises 516 metres giving an average gradient slightly steeper than 1 in 5 but rising to more than 1 in 3 in places.

The ten minute journey takes passengers to Rosshütte which is a focal point for skiers or walkers according to season with a cafe and toilets. From here a cable car leads straight up to the summit of the Seefelder Joch which at 2,074 metres stands some 300 metres above the terminus of the railway. Another, longer cable car, crosses the Hermannstal to reach the Härmelekopf.

The two funicular cars accommodate up to 100 people. Summer service from mid May until mid October is half hourly from 9.00 until 17.00 with no 12.30 departures. There is however an 8.30 service on Saturdays and Sundays.

The Winter timetable from mid December to mid April offers a quarter hourly frequency between 9.00 and 16.30. The line does not operate during the gaps between the two seasons.

The journey is expensive. In March 1992 it cost 120s return from Seefeld to Rosshütte or 150s including one of the cable cars. Most of the customers were skiers travelling on their lift passes. It is an adventure to be undertaken on a fine day if possible.

Looking up towards the summit of the funicular on 27 March 1992. *(Philippa Simpson)*

The view north west from Rosshütte towards the Wettersteingebirge which mark the border with Germany. This helps explain why the railway to Reutte in Tirol had to be so indirect.
(Philippa Simpson)

The Zillertal Bahn

'Neue Austro Takt' on the Zillertalbahn. One of the hourly dmus approaching Uderns bound for
Mayrhofen on 21 August 1993. *(Martin Bairstow)*

Linking the holiday ski resort of Mayrhofen with the ÖBB main line at Jenbach, the 76cm gauge Zillertalbahn combines the function of a tourist facility with that of an everyday working railway. 32km in length, the single track meanders along the glaciated valley, never far from the parallel road.

The Zillertalbahn AG was formed in December 1899 after two decades of proposal and counter proposal.

Opening took place in stages:

Jenbach – Fügen	20.12.1900
Fügen – Kaltenbach	24. 2.1901
Kaltenbach – Erlach	26. 5.1901
Erlach – Zell am Ziller	21. 7.1901
Zell am Ziller – Mayrhofen	31. 7.1902

The timetable from 1 August 1902 offered departures from Mayrhofen at 5.32am, 11.34am, 2.32pm and 5.56pm with an extra on Sundays and holidays at 7.32pm. All trains conveyed second and third class carriages and the journey took just under two hours.

In 1928 the line acquired its first diesel railcar. This had been ordered the year before. Because of the delay in delivery, the manufacturers made available a diesel loco, the first on the Austrian narrow gauge. This ran on the Zillertalbahn from August 1927 working passenger trains in Summer only because it had no heating equipment. In 1930

it was purchased by the Federal Railways and is still shunting at Waidhofen a.d. Ybbs in Upper Austria as ÖBB No 2090 001.

In the mid 1950s the Zillertalbahn was threatened by the new road being built through the valley. The Provincial Government of the Tirol and the local authorities purchased a majority of the share capital in the Railway Company whose name was changed in July 1956 to Zillertaler Verkehrsbetriebe AG (Ziller Valley Transport Company) to reflect the organisation's expanding interest in bus operation.

The line was relaid during the 1960s with heavier rail which has allowed higher speeds. Radio signalling was introduced in 1971 allowing the whole line to be controlled from Jenbach.

The 1972 Summer timetable showed seven trains each way daily – four of them dmus including an express taking under an hour – the remainder loco hauled taking an hour and a quarter for the through journey.

With the introduction of 'Neue Austro Takt' in 1991, the Zillertalbahn entered into the full spirit of things by recasting its timetable to give hourly departures from Jenbach between 6.50am and 6.50pm and from Mayrhofen between 7.20am and 7.20pm providing consistently good connections to and from Innsbruck. As the single journey takes just under an hour, three diesel trains are required to work the regular interval service passing one another at Schlitters and Zell am Ziller respectively at 2 and 33 minutes past each hour.

Most services are worked by dmus, purpose built for the line since 1985, but diesel loco hauled trains also feature with modern coaches similar to the dmu vehicles.

General freight is carried both in narrow gauge wagons and in standard gauge vehicles mounted on transporters. There is a large traffic in timber from the yard at Fügen-Hart.

A steam tourist train runs during the Summer twice each way daily. This is over and above the hourly diesel service. In 1993, the morning train at 10.30 from Jenbach and 12.47 from Mayrhofen ran from 1 May to 24 October and over the 12 days of Christmas plus Easter weekend. The afternoon train at 2.55 from Jenbach and 5.00 from Mayrhofen ran only during the Summer timetable.

The steam train is available at a supplementary fare but the number of individual customers appears comparatively small. On our trip in August 1993, all such patrons were confined to the front vehicle of the 17 coach train. The rest of the train was reserved for coach parties who joined and left at various intermediate stations. Few of them seemed to travel any appreciable distance. They just took the train ride in one direction only as part of a day long coach trip, their fleet of buses running empty on the parallel road for that part of the journey.

There was something of a party atmosphere on parts of the train with live music and alcoholic refreshments being dispensed in some carriages.

Our journey on Saturday 21 August was something of a disaster. We left Jenbach at 10.30 behind 0-6-2T No 5 'Gerlos'. We were booked to be overtaken at Kaltenbach-Stumm by the 10.50 dmu ex Jenbach. The through journey should have occupied 1 hour 40 minutes against 57 minutes by diesel.

On this occasion we were overtaken first at Schlitters where we had to shunt forward and back to allow two dmus to pass each other as well as us. We then lost more time all the way. Evidently our 17 coach load was too much for No 5 which had to be assisted by a diesel loco from Kaltenbach-Stumm onwards. We were overtaken again at Zell am Ziller by the 11.50 ex Jenbach finally reaching Mayrhofen at 1pm. It had taken 2 1/2 hours to travel 20 miles on hard seats. The only credit one could give to the Zillertalbahn was that they had endeavoured to keep the diesel service on schedule by holding the steam train at every loop.

We returned by dmu which was a very different experience, faster and altogether more business like. We got a better view from the more panoramic side windows though, unfortunately, these dmus do not give any forward or rear view. With passengers joining and leaving, with tidy stations whether manned or unstaffed, with freight in private sidings and in the exchange yard at Jenbach, the Zillertalbahn typifies what a narrow gauge branch line should and can be.

'Rabbit Cards', 'Umwelt Tickets' and most ÖBB facilities are valid on the diesel service on the Zillertalbahn.

0-6-2T No 5 'Gerlos', built 1930, prepares to leave Jenbach on what turned out to be a rather slow progress to Mayrhofen on 21 August 1993. The connecting 'Trans Alpin' set which had brought us from Kirchberg is just visible.
(Martin Bairstow)

0-6-2T No 3 'Tirol' passing the timber yard at Fügen-Hart with the afternoon Jenbach to Mayrhofen tourist train on 26 June 1992. The loco is a veteran of 1902. *(David Beeken)*

Timber being loaded onto a standard gauge wagon which is standing on 76cm gauge 'rollbocke' in the siding at Fügen-Hart. *(David Beeken)*

Catering department vehicle at Jenbach in June 1991.
(Martin Bairstow)

Dmu No VTI approaching Zell am Ziller from Mayrhofen on 8 June 1991. This three coach creation began life with only two vehicles in 1955 on the metre gauge branch of the DB between Ravensburg and Bainfurt. When that closed in 1961, the unit was regauged to 1,062mm in order to run on a non-electrified section of the Rotterdam Tramways where it acquired the centre generator coach. It came to the Zillertalbahn in 1967 where it was again regauged to 760mm. It has retired since 1991 with the delivery of further new dmu stock.
(Martin Bairstow)

A Mayrhofen bound dmu pauses at Ramsberg-Hippach on 28 June 1992.
(David Beeken)

Diesel loco haulage of passenger trains has been rendered comparatively rare by the acquisition of additional multiple units. B-B (0-4-4-0) No D10 prepares to leave Mayrhofen with the 9.20 for Jenbach on 28 June 1992. The loco was built in 1970 for the JZ (Jugoslavian Railways)
(David Beeken)

The Achensee Bahn

0-4-0 No 2 connects with the 'St. Benedikt' at Achensee Seespitz on 4 July 1992.   *(David Beeken)*

This 7km part rack, part adhesion line climbs out of the Inn Valley at Jenbach to reach the Southern tip of Achensee. It was opened in 1889 and manages to operate with just three out of its original four 0-4-0 steam locomotives. As on similar mountain lines, the engine boilers lean forward at 1 in 20 as part compensation for the prevailing gradient.

Perhaps the singular feature of the Achenseebahn is that the engine does not simply push its train up to the summit of a mountain like the Schafberg and Schneeberg lines in Austria, or the Rothorn in Switzerland or even the Snowdon Mountain Railway in Wales. Half way along its journey the Achensee loco runs round the train and leads it **downhill** towards the lakeside, the 1 in 20 tilt on the engine compounding the 1 in 40 gradient on the track.

The metre gauge line starts alongside the ÖBB in Jenbach Station on the opposite side to the Zillertalbahn. Here are found the loco works, carriage shed and offices as well as a small museum. As the loco propels the train out of Jenbach, the conductor rides on the front platform

from where he pulls a rope to sound the engine whistle at level crossings.

Beyond the halt at Burgeck, the gradient stiffens to 1 in 6. Passengers can enjoy a view over the Inn Valley towards the Stubaier Alpen and the Wilder Kaiser. As the ascent continues, there are views of the Zillertal.

After climbing for 30 minutes, the train reaches Eben where the loco runs round for the descent towards the lake.

Originally the line terminated some 600 metres from the steamer landing stage. This gap was filled by a 60cm track upon which luggage and goods were conveyed. This situation lasted until 1916 when the 60cm track was requisitioned by the military making way for the railway itself to be extended. The new station building and landing stage were completed in 1929.

The train service is seasonal with six advertised return trips daily between May and September. As the maximum load is two coaches, two trains may run in one timetable path at busy times. The 'Rabbit Card' is valid.

0-4-0T No 3 waits departure from Jenbach on 26 June 1992.   *(David Beeken)*

No 3 attacks the first gradient away from the main line on 22 August 1987.   *(John Holroyd)*

An ascending train makes an impressive sight and sound, just above Jenbach on a very wet 24 August 1993. *(Martin Bairstow)*

Achenseebahn No. 1 has arrived at the lakeside terminus in August 1973. *(Stuart Baker)*

The Achensee Steamers

The oldest vessel, 'St Josef', predates the Railway by two years. It was built in 1887 for the Fiecht Monastery which then owned the lake. The City of Innsbruck assisted with a loan. Carrying 120 passengers, the 'St Josef' is still in service though it was converted from steam to diesel power in 1950.

A second slightly larger ship called 'St Benedikt' entered service in 1889, the year the Railway opened. It ran for 70 years, steam powered to the end, but was replaced in 1959 by a new diesel ship of the same name. This has capacity for 300 passengers.

The third and largest member of the fleet is the 'Stadt Innsbruck'. This entered service in 1912 under the name 'Stella Maris' (star of the sea). It was the first motor ship on any European inland lake. It carries up to 400 passengers and can manage a speed of 15mph.

The change of name was a result of the transfer of ownership of the lake and its steamers to the City of Innsbruck in 1919. Five years later, the steamers were vested in the present owners, the Tiroler Wasserkraftwerke AG, who are also majority shareholders in the Achenseebahn.

The service is seasonal operating from early May to the end of October. The journey from the railway station at Seespitz (Head of Lake) to Scholastika takes 55 minutes with four stops including Pertisau where the vessels are berthed overnight. The timetable is based generally on train connections with six return trips along the full length of the lake plus two short workings between Pertisau and Scholastika. During May and October the frequency is about half this level with only one ship operating.

The return fare on the steamer in 1993 was 110 Schillings. There are through bookings affording some discount from various ÖBB stations in the Tirol and also from the Zillertalbahn. If you use a 'Rabbit Card' to reach Achensee Seespitz by train, then you will have to pay normal fare on the ship.

The 'Stadt Innsbruck' in service on Achensee. When it stops at an intermediate pier, its motors shut down but are restarted by compressed air when it is ready to depart again. *(John Holroyd)*

The well appointed forward saloon aboard the 'Stadt Innsbruck'. *(Martin Bairstow)*

The oldest ship in the fleet, the 'St Josef', built 1887, moored at Pertisau on 22 August 1987.

(John Holroyd)

And the newest. The 1959 'St. Benedikt' at Seespitz on 6 June 1991.

(Martin Bairstow)

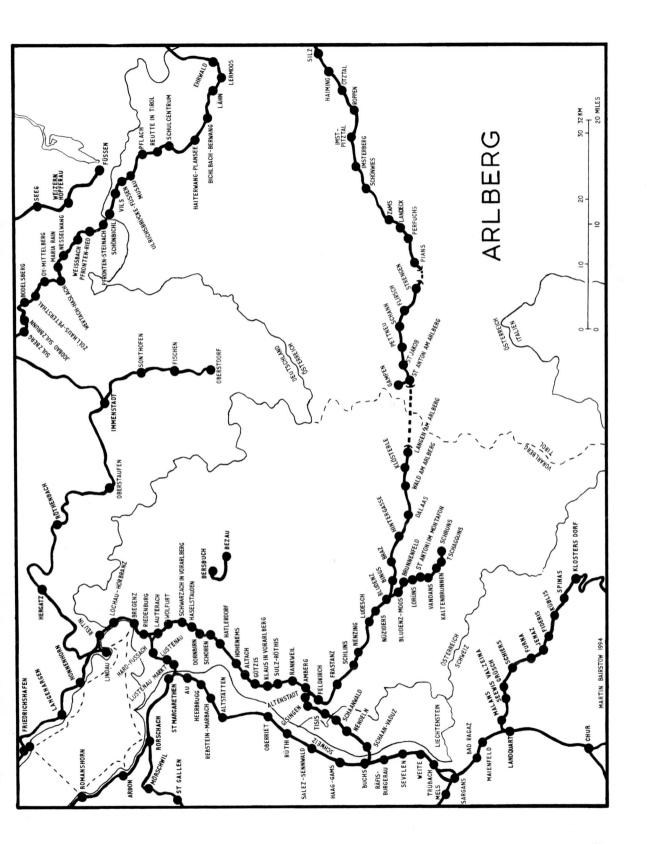

ARLBERG

SILZ
ÖTZTAL
HAIMING
ROPPEN
IMST-PITZTAL
IMSTERBERG
SCHÖNWIES
ZAMS
LANDECK
PERFUCHS
PIANS
STRENGEN
FLIRSCH
SCHANN
PETTNEU
GAMPEN
ST JAKOB
ST ANTON AM ARLBERG
LANGEN AM ARLBERG
WALD AM ARLBERG
KLÖSTERLE
DALAAS
HINTERGASSE
BRAZ
BINGS
BLUDENZ
BRUNNENFELD
BLUDENZ-MOOS
ST ANTON IM MONTAFON
LORÜNS
VANDANS
SCHRUNS
TSCHAGGUNS
KALTENBRUNNEN
NÜZIDERS
LUDESCH
NENZING
SCHLINS
FRASTANZ
AMBERG
FELDKIRCH
ALTENSTADT
GISINGEN
TISIS
SCHAANWALD
NENDELN
SCHAAN-VADUZ

EHRWALD
LERMOOS
LÄHN
BICHLBACH-BERWANG
HAITERWANG-PLANSEE
SCHULCENTRUM
REUTTE IN TIROL
VILS
PFLACH
MUSAU
ULRICHSBRÜCKE-FÜSSEN
SCHÖNBICHL
PFRONTEN-STEINACH
PFRONTEN-RIED
NESSELWANG
MARIA RAIN
WEISSBACH
OY-MITTELBERG
BODELSBERG
WERTACH-HASLACH
ZOLLHAUS-PETERSTHAL
JOJBAD SULZBRUNN
SULZBERG

FÜSSEN
SEEG
WEIZERN-HOPFERAU

DEUTSCHLAND
ÖSTERREICH

VORARLBERG
TIROL

ÖSTERREICH
ITALIEN

SONTHOFEN
FISCHEN
OBERSTDORF
IMMENSTADT
OBERSTAUFEN
RÖTHENBACH

HERGATZ
REUTIN
LOCHAU-HÖRBRANZ
BREGENZ
RIEDENBURG
LAUTERACH
WOLFURT
SCHWARZACH IN VORARLBERG
DORNBIRN
HASELSTAUDEN
SCHOREN
HATLERDORF
HOHENEMS
ALTACH
GÖTZIS
KLAUS IN VORARLBERG
SULZ-RÖTHIS
RANKWEIL

BEZAU
BERSBUCH

FRIEDRICHSHAFEN
LANGENARGEN
NONNENHORN
LINDAU
HARD-FUSSACH
LUSTENAU
LUSTENAU MARKT
AU
HEERBRUGG
REBSTEIN-MARBACH
ALTSTÄTTEN
ST MARGARETHEN
RORSCHACH
MÖRSCHWIL
ST GALLEN
ARBON
ROMANSHORN

OBERRIET
RÜTHI
SALEZ-SENNWALD
HAAG-GAMS
RÄFIS-BURGERAU
BUCHS
SEVELEN
TRÜBBACH
WEITE
MELS
SARGANS
LIECHTENSTEIN

SCHWEIZ
ÖSTERREICH

BAD RAGAZ
MAIENFELD
LANDQUART
MALANS
SEEWIS-GRÜSCH
VALZEINA
SCHIERS
FURNA
JENAZ
FIDERIS
KÜBLIS
SPINAS
KLOSTERS DORF
CHUR

MARTIN BAIRSTOW 1994

30 KM 32 KM
20 MILES
0 10 20

69

Die Innsbrucker Verkehrsbetriebe

The Innsbruck Transport Service

When the line from Innsbruck to Hall in Tirol closed in 1974, it was feared that the remainder of the tramway network might follow. Instead, the system has been modernised using second hand rolling stock from Germany. Two light railways, the Mittelgebirgsbahn and the Stubaitalbahn, have been made compatible so that services may operate through to the centre of the City.

The urban tramway system is a modest affair comprising two routes, each about two miles in length. Route No. 1 starts at the lower station of the Hungerburgbahn funicular, passes outside the Hauptbahnhof, runs past the Westbahnhof and terminates at Bergisel where the main depot is situated. In the return direction, the trams do not serve the Hauptbahnhof but pass along Maria Theresien Strasse.

Route No. 3 runs from Amras to the Hauptbahnhof where the trams do not terminate but continue round the City Centre loop via Maria Theresien Strasse and back to Amras.

All the lines are double track, metre gauge, laid in the centre of the roadway and electrified at 600 volts dc. Service frequency on routes 1 and 3 is every six minutes Monday to Friday from early morning until 8pm, thereafter every $^1/_4$ hour. Weekend service is only slightly less intensive.

The network was built in the period 1905 to 1908. The route numbers were allocated in about 1911. The missing No. 2 ran to Mühlau but was withdrawn about 1920. it was effectively a short working along the Innsbruck-Hall in Tirol Lokalbahn. This was a 12km line which began life as a steam tramway in 1891. It was electrified in 1909 becoming route No. 4. It operated until 9 June 1974 when it fell victim to road alterations in connection with the 1976 Winter Olympics.

Route No. 5 was a circular service which operated around the 6 City Centre during the 1920s and 30s. No. 6 was allocated to the Mittelgebirgsbahn when that was electrified in 1936 (see next item). The tramway system was operated by the Innsbruck-Hall in Tirol Company which in 1943 changed its name to the Innsbrucker Verkehrsbetriebe to reflect its growing interest in bus as well as tram service.

Double articulated ex Bielefeld No 51 picks up a customer outside the Hauptbahnhof on a rather inclement 24 March 1992. It will follow the No 1 route to Bergisel then take to the mountains.

(Martin Bairstow)

No 42 negotiates its way along Maria Theresien Strasse en route from Bergisel to the Hungerburgbahn. Route No 1 does not pass the Hauptbahnhof in this direction.
(Martin Bairstow)

Vanished attraction. A motor coach leaves Innsbruck Hauptbahnhof with two 4 wheel trailers on the No 4 tram route to Solbad Hall. This closed in 1974. Trams now only run in one direction outside the Hauptbahnhof – clockwise. *(Douglas Butterfield)*

Nos 53 and 39 pass at the Stubaitalbahnhof on 27 August 1993. Bergisel terminus is the next stop just to the right of the Church. The Stubaitalbahn branches off in front of the two trams.   *(Martin Bairstow)*

Tram 76 at Pradler Friedhof, the penultimate stop on the No 3 Amras service.   *(Martin Bairstow)*

The Mittelgebirgs Bahn

Innsbruck – Igls

Mittelgebirgsbahn No 2 prepares to leave Bergisel for Igls with two ancient trailers on 10 August 1973. Tram No 66, also now withdrawn, has worked the connecting No 1 service. *(Stuart Baker)*

The resort of Igls is reached by the No 6 tram which nowadays leaves hourly from the Hungerburgbahn proceeding on exactly the same route as the No 1 through the City until it reaches Bergisel. There it waits for the incoming tram to clear the single line section before setting off on the 8.4km Mittelgebirgsbahn. Climbing at a maximum gradient of 1 in 22 it rises a total of 271 metres.

The line opened on 26 June 1900 and was worked by three 0-6-2 tank engines supplied by Krauss of Linz. It was electrified at 1,000 volts dc in 1936 using three motor coaches transferred from the Innsbruck – Hall in Tirol Lokalbahn. Assisted by the original trailers, these maintained the service until 1983 when the line was finally integrated into the Innsbruck tram system.

An hourly service operates to Igls leaving Bergisel between 5.30am and 7.30pm with all but the first two starting from the Hungerburgbahn and running via the Hauptbahnhof.

A single tram ticket is very expensive for the distance covered – 18 schillings in 1993. Better value for the tourist was the one zone day ticket (Tagesnetzkarte) covering tram routes, 1, 3 and 6 as far as Tantegert. This cost 25s but you needed a two zone ticket at 33s to go to Igls. These could be bought from drivers. These tickets were also valid on buses and trolleybuses. Regular commuters have various period passes available.

Much of the journey to Igls is through forest. Tantegert station is a passing loop used only when the hourly service is augmented. After leaving here, the tram could be heard for some time screeching its way round the many reverse curves higher up the line.
(Martin Bairstow)

The intermediate stations on the single line all have platforms on both sides because the single ended rolling stock only has doors on the right hand side. Aldrans looking towards Igls.
(Martin Bairstow)

Igls terminus on 27 August 1993. No 42 has gone round the turning circle and is now facing back towards Innsbruck.
(Martin Bairstow)

The tram fleet in normal service comes from the German City of Bielefeld, where the tramways have been upgraded to metro status with some underground sections. They are single ended as there are turning circles at all termini. Eleven of them, Nos 31-41 are now six axle vehicles but two more, Nos 51 and 52 are still in eight axle double articulated formation. These work largely on the Igls service.

The Hungerburg Bahn

Operated by the IVB, the Hungerburgbahn is a funicular dating from 12 September 1906. 837 metres in length, it climbs 290 metres crossing the River Inn on a viaduct. It was substantially rebuilt in 1958 with new carriages conveying 90 passengers each. These, in turn, were replaced in 1982 by the present pair of vehicles which also accommodate 90 passengers plus the 'driver'.

The service operates every 15 minutes from 6.55am until 7.55pm. There is an intermediate stop at the Alpenzoo just below the half way passing loop. At Hungerburg, passengers may change on to the Nordkettenbahn, a cable car in two sections which will whisk them up a further 1,400 metres to the summit at Hafelekar (2,260 metres above sea level).

The Hungerburg funicular begins its ascent from the No 1 tram terminus by crossing the River Inn on this viaduct. The fortifications at the bottom of the piers are a protection against debris floating down the river.
(Martin Bairstow)

75

The Stubaital Bahn

Innsbruck – Fulpmes

Steeply graded, heavily engineered and sharply curved, the 20km Stubaitalbahn winds its way between Innsbruck and Fulpmes. The hour long journey begins outside the Hauptbahnhof and follows the route of the No 1 and No 6 trams as far as the Stubaitalbahnhof, the stop before Bergisel. Here the Fulpmes train swings off the road into the station area which was, prior to 2 July 1983, the terminus of the Stubaitalbahn.

Once onto its own track and under the authority of radio signalling, the Fulpmes train begins to climb very steeply. It turns through 90 degrees then enters the 160 metre Kehrtunnel which takes it back through 180 degrees.

The line was built at the beginning of the century. A proportion of the cost was subscribed by the Union Electricity Company on condition that it was electrified using industrial frequency ac overhead in preference to the third rail dc system which had been under consideration. The rest of the capital came from national and local public funds. The line opened on Sunday 1 August 1904. It was operated by the Innsbruck – Hall in Tirol Lokalbahn, predecessor of the IVB. Today the line is owned exclusively by the City of Innsbruck. Rolling stock is in similar livery to the IVB but the name Stubaitalbahn A G is still used. Since 1983 the

service has operated at the rather strange interval of every 50 minutes. The last train from Innsbruck to Fulpmes is at 7.40pm but there are three later trips as far as Mutters.

IVB day tickets, mentioned in the previous chapter, are not valid on the Stubaitalbahn except for local journeys on the town section where it shares the tram tracks. Most ÖBB facilities are valid, however, including the 'Rabbit Card' and 'Umwelt Ticket'.

Tickets are bought from a conductor who sits at a little desk towards the rear of the double articulated train set. This and the corresponding empty desk near the front for when the train is going the other way, combine to use up a lot of space and there are only 61 seats per three section train. There is, however, official standing room for 93 further passengers.

Numbered 81 to 88, each train comprises two end sections which came from Hagen, in Germany, where the tramways closed in 1976. They had run there as six axle single articulated units but have been lengthened whilst in Innsbruck by the insertion of central sections taken out of ex Bielefeld trams.

Two original Stubaitalbahn motor coaches, Nos 2 and 3 are retained with a fleet of trailers. They can now work off the d.c. system and are used on special workings.

No 3 + trailers at the Stubaitalbahnhof on 10 August 1973 waiting to depart for Fulpmes. The track on the left connects on to the Innsbruck tram system and is now used in normal service. *(Stuart Baker)*

A line for all seasons. The crew find it too hot to wear their jackets on arrival at Fulpmes on 28 June 1992.

(David Beeken)

Somewhat in contrast, on 24 March 1992 veteran motor coach No 2 has just run round its trailers by the time honoured gravity system. Its special excursion customers cannot wait to get on board but they will be frustrated when No 83 encounters a blockage on the line leaving them stuck at Fulpmes.

(Martin Bairstow)

No 81 waits for custom outside the Hauptbahnhof in August 1993. The train does not reverse here but performs a circuit of the City Centre via Maria Theresien Strasse.
(Martin Bairstow)

Luxury travel on the 1904 Stubaitalbahn stock.
(Stuart Baker)

Disaster. On 24 March 1992, our train from Fulpmes came to a stand 400 metres short of Luimes Halt because a tree had brought down the overhead wires. We had to climb down the embankment and walk to Luimes, to which point No 84 had been authorised to travel. Normally it would have waited to pass us at Telfeser Wiesen but radio control gives the flexibility to accommodate emergencies. The two trains, 400 metres apart exchanged passengers. We were only delayed 20 minutes. After this, the line was closed between Mutters and Fulpmes and a bus operated whilst repairs were carried out. *(Martin Bairstow)*

Standseilbahnen – Funiculars

Generally speaking, not even rack railways can climb much above 1 in 4. The Pilatusbahn in Switzerland is exceptional at almost 1 in 2. A funicular can go even steeper. The Piotta – Piora line in Switzerland reaches a maximum gradient of 878 ⁰/₀₀ (1 in 1.14) which is almost vertical.

There is nothing quite as steep as that in Austria though there are a number of funiculars in the Tirol. The Hungerburg and Rosshütte lines have already been featured.

A funicular is a railway worked by a cable. There are usually two carriages linked by a steel cable which passes through a winding mechanism at the upper station. The line is single track with a passing loop half way. The carriage wheels have double flanges on one side and none at the other which explains how they always know which way to go at the passing loop which has no moveable points. Because of the gradient the carriages are stepped so that the passengers remain more or less vertical.

The Arlberg – Kandahar Bahn starts at the back of St Anton Station. It is of standard gauge and was opened in 1972. 1,414 metres in length it rises at a maximum of just under 1 in 2 to gain 533 metres in height. From the upper station at Gampen, there is a cable car which will take you a further 476 metres to the summit of the Kampall.

According to the Austrian timetable, there is a service only in the winter ski season but the funicular was certainly working in August 1993.

The Hartkaiserbahn, also built in 1972, uses identical rolling stock to the line at St Anton. Each carriage accommodates up to 120 passengers in five compartments. The line climbs 706 metres in a length of 2.3km. The lower station at Ellmau can be reached by bus from St Johann.

The Olympiabahn is 2,105 metres in length. Situated on the outskirts of Innsbruck, it takes its name from the 1976 Winter Olympics. The gauge is

The Arlberg-Kandahar funicular in service on 26 August 1993.   *(Martin Bairstow)*

1427mm, just less than standard. To avoid getting blocked by snow, the line is built on a elevated structure the whole length from Axamer Lizum to Hoadl. The service is hourly with extras as required.

All 'Inter City' as well as other Austrian trains carry names. In Austrian Railway Group Journal No. 8, Iain and Mike Parsons attempted to explain the origin of 136 Austrian train names. 21 of them are mountains, including 'Hahnenkamm'. The latest carriages carry the names on roller blinds but older stock relies on metal signs which tend to get bashed about a little.   *(Iain Parsons)*

Driver's eye view from 399.01 approaching Neukirchen am Grossvenediger bound for Krimml on 23 August 1987 *(John Holroyd)*

'Window on Austria'. A passenger's view of Achensee from the saloon of the steamer 'Stadt Innsbruck'. *(John Holroyd)*